THE GREAT

THAI
COOKBOOK

Photography by Peter Barry
Recipes by Jacqueline Bellefontaine
Watercolour illustrations by Sally Brewer
Designed by Alison Lee, Julie Smith and Helen Johnson
Edited by Jillian Stewart and Kate Cranshaw

4059 The Great Thai Cookbook
This edition published in 1997 by CLB
Distributed in the USA by BHB International Inc.,
30 Edison Drive, Wayne, New Jersey 07470
© 1995 CLB International, Godalming, Surrey, England
Color separations by Advance Laser Graphic Arts, Hong Kong
Printed and bound in Singapore
All rights reserved
ISBN 1-85833-334-2

THE GREAT
THAI
COOKBOOK

JACQUELINE BELLEFONTAINE

Contents

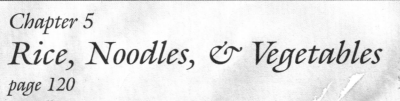

Introduction

Thai food is a wonderful and exciting amalgam of flavors and styles resulting in a cuisine, which, although influenced by several other countries, is quite unique to Thailand.

It is little wonder that Thai food is becoming more and more popular in the West. It isn't just the delicious flavors that are becoming known. Thai cooking is so perfect for our changing lifestyle. Not only is it quick to prepare and cook, many dishes taking only minutes to produce, it is also a healthy cuisine in which fresh vegetables play a predominant part. In addition, oil is generally used only in small quantities and fish and chicken are more important ingredients than red meats.

Authentic Thai food can easily be produced at home and with its many different styles of cooking – stir-frying, steaming, roasting, and barbecuing – it need never become uninteresting either. Similarities with both Chinese and Indian cuisine are easily recognized, though generally speaking, Thai food is hotter and spicier than Chinese and the long simmering times characteristic of many Indian curries are absent.

Most of the ingredients used in Thai cooking are now easy to find, especially if you have a good Oriental food store close at hand. The ingredients most commonly used have been listed on pages 12-15 and will soon help you to familiarize yourself with the less well-known food items.

The Regions

Geographically, Thailand can be divided into four very different major regions. This produces a cuisine with strong regional variations.

The North

This rugged mountainous region shares its border with Myanmar (Burma) and Laos, whose own cuisines have influenced some northern dishes. Sticky rice is preferred to the fluffier, fragrant rice more common elsewhere in Thailand. In contrast to the more usual method of eating rice, sticky rice is formed into balls with the fingers and eaten after dipping in sauces and curries. Coconut milk is not as popular in dishes from the north. Although some foods are highly seasoned,

the curries are generally milder than those of the central and northeast regions. A hot chili dip will nevertheless always be available for those who love spicy foods.

The Northeast

Although this region covers almost one third of Thailand and consists of seven of the most heavily-populated provinces, the soil in the northeast is poor and in many places only yields a subsistence living for farmers. The region suffers from prolonged droughts, and when the rain finally falls the result is often heavy flooding. Temperatures, too, can be extreme and despite the considerable agricultural progress and modernization in farming methods, real hardship is still prevalent. Spicy meat dishes (Laab) are a specialty, although they tend to be reserved for special occasions as meat is often scarce in many areas. Freshwater fish and shrimp are the main protein sources. The cuisine is very hot and spicy and chilies are used in vast quantities, perhaps to help mask the sometimes poor quality of the ingredients.

The Central Plains

In great contrast to the infertile soil of the northeast, the central plains are a fertile expanse of flat farmland, protected on three sides by mountains. The area is veined with rivers and canals which irrigate the land, and it is here the world-renowned fragrant rice, sometimes known as jasmine rice, is grown for home use and for export. The fertile soil also yields abundant crops of fruits and vegetables. Dishes are usually accompanied by fragrant rice steamed and served plain or mixed with other ingredients. Basil, garlic, and coriander (cilantro) are popular flavorings. Coconut milk is also used lavishly in the cuisine of this region. Bangkok, the capital, is also the biggest city of the central plains. It is a meeting-point for many other cultures, and so many of the dishes of this region reflect the influences of other countries, while retaining a unique Thai flavor of their own.

The South

The South consists of narrow peninsula snaking like a long twisted finger down to Malaysia. Traveling down its length, orchards, truck farms, and rice fields give way to plantations of rubber trees and coconut palms. Not surprisingly, coconut milk is used in many of the dishes from the south, and coconut oil is the most

popular fat for sautéing and frying. With two coastlines totalling 1,625 miles in length, there is a rich abundance of seafood. The majority of Thailand's moslem population lives in the south. Their cuisine bears clear signs of Indian influences in such dishes as Mussaman curry. Raw vegetables are served with most meals and the cuisine is very spicy, although perhaps not quite as hot as the dishes from the northeast. The tropical climate yields an abundance of beautiful and exotic tropical fruits, such as star fruit (carambola), jackfruit and the evil-smelling durian.

Cooking Techniques

There is nothing difficult about Thai-style cooking, nor is there any need to buy lots of special equipment. Stir-frying, steaming, boiling, and frying are the main methods of cooking.

Equipment

A wok (Kata) is the most frequently-used cooking utensil and although a large skillet can be used, it is worthwhile investing in this inexpensive piece of equipment if you enjoy Oriental-style foods.

The addition of a bamboo steamer, which is placed directly in the wok, is useful but you can improvise by placing a plate or colander over a saucepan of gently simmering water and covering it with a lid to prevent the steam escaping.

Thais use a wire-mesh basket on a bamboo handle for lifting foods out of the pan, but a slotted draining spoon or skimmer serves just as well.

You will also need a couple of saucepans and some sharp knives. Thai cooks use a large meat cleaver for most food preparation, even the intricate carvings of garnishes used on special occasions, but you will probably find it easier and safer to employ a good cook's knife.

A pestle and mortar is a necessity if you intend to prepare your own curry pastes. A food processor is generally unable to cope with the small quantities of spices used, although an electric spice-grinder or coffee-grinder works well, and cuts down on preparation time.

Stir-Frying

The secret of good stir-frying is to cook the ingredients quickly over a high heat, keeping the food constantly on the move to prevent it from burning. The high sides of a wok allow a large amount of food to be stirred whilst cooking without the food flying out of the pan. The ingredients should be added in quick succession, so it is essential to do all of the food preparation before you start cooking. Indeed, you will find that most of the time spent making these dishes is taken up by the preparation.

Preparing the Ingredients

Some of the food items used in Thai cooking need special preparation before use. Here is how to prepare and use some of the less familiar ingredients:

Chilies

Unless you live in the southwest, you may not be used to handling chilies. Their juice is strongly irritant, so it is a good idea to wear disposable or rubber gloves when slicing them [1]. In all cases, wash your hands after preparing them, as even a tiny amount of the juice can cause considerable discomfort if it comes into contact with your eyes or mouth. If you prefer a milder flavor, discard the seeds [2] which contain much of the heat and remember that, generally speaking, the smaller the chili the stronger it will be. If you do not like your food too hot, you can still enjoy Thai food just be sparing with the chilies, or use larger, milder varieties.

Coconut Milk

If you cannot find unsweetened coconut milk in the stores, you can make your own by combining ½ cup unsweetened shredded coconut with 4 cups warm water, milk, or half milk-half water. Stir well or process in a blender for a few seconds. Allow to stand for 20 minutes, then strain through cheesecloth, squeezing out as much liquid as you can.

Fish Sauce

If you can't find authentic Thai or Vietnamese fish sauce, make you own substitute by pounding together a can of drained anchovy fillets with 1 tbsp sugar. Add a 3 tbsps soy sauce. Allow to stand for at least 30 minutes, then strain before using.

Fresh Root Ginger

Peel or scrape the skin from the root, then slice, chop, or grate as required [3].

Lemongrass

To use, cut away the grassy top and hard root [4]. Remove and discard the tough outer leaves. Bruise the stem to release the flavor by pressing hard beneath the flat blade of a knife, or thinly slice the central core [5].

Tamarind

The juice needs to be extracted from tamarind pulp before use. To do this, soak about 1 part tamarind in 2 parts warm water for about 20-30 minutes, mashing occasionally against the side of the bowl or pitcher. Strain through a sieve, forcing the juice out of the pulp with the back of a spoon [6]. Scrape the underside of the sieve and add this pulp to the liquid. Tamarind juice is best used the same day.

Garnishes

Thais believe that food must please the eye, nose, and tastebuds and they take great care in food presentation of dishes, all of which are usually garnished, even if only with a sprig or sprinkling of coriander (cilantro). Garnishing will increase the enjoyment of your meal and in the following section you will find a guide to preparing a number of simple garnishes used throughout the book.

1

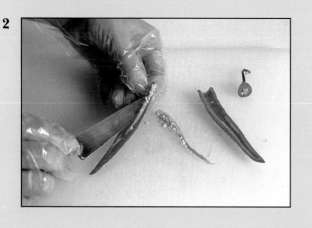

2

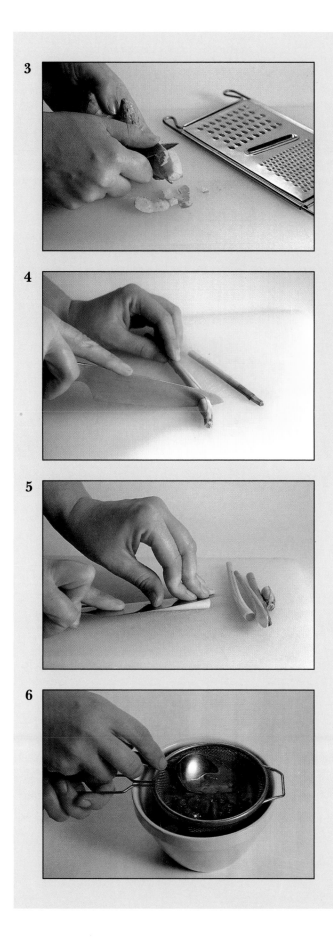

How to Make Simple Garnishes

Chili "Flowers"

These are made by cutting two or more times through the chili from the tip almost to the base. Place the chili on a chopping board and hold at the stem. Use a sharp knife to make the lengthwise cuts [1]. Place in a bowl of ice water [2] and leave for about 1 hour or until required. The ends of the chili will curl outward to produce a flowerlike effect [3]. The flowers can be made with large or small chilies. Removing the seeds will also help the ends to curl.

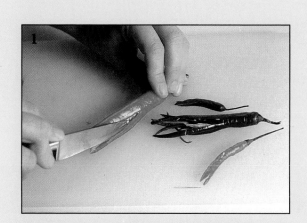

Spring Onion "Brushes"

1
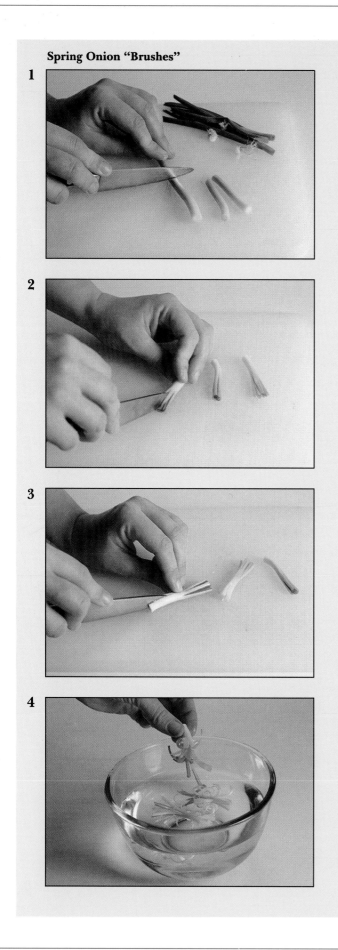

2

3

4

Chili and Green Onion (Scallion) Curls

1

Carrot "Twigs"

1
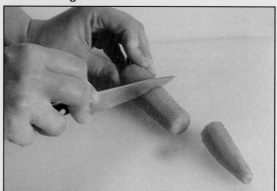

2
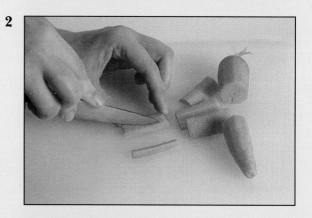

3
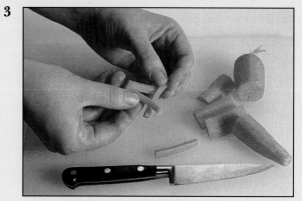

Green Onion (Scallion) "Brushes"

A similar effect to chili "flowers" can be achieved with green onions (scallions). First, trim away the top, leaving a piece about 2-3 inches long. Trim away the root [1]. Make cuts from the green end, but leave the bulb joined at the tip [2]. Alternatively, make smaller cuts at each end which do not quite meet in the middle [3]. Place in ice water for at least 30 minutes. When you remove them, shake off the excess water. The ends will have curled to form attractive brushes [4].

Chili and Green Onion (Scallion) Curls

These make an attractive topping. Trim the chili stem, trim and discard the root and top part of green onion (scallion). Shred both vegetables. Place them in ice water until they curl [1].

Carrot "Twigs"

Cut a 2-inch section from a carrot [1], then slice it thinly lengthwise into rectangles. Take one slice of the carrot and make a cut from each end almost through to the opposite end [2]. Twist the two outer strips so that they cross over [3]. Repeat with the remaining carrot slices. You can also make "twigs" from citrus rind or slices of cucumber.

Banana Leaves

These are often cut into attractive shapes and used to line a platter or for garnish. If using, wipe clean and cut into the desired shape with scissors.

Planning and Serving a Thai Meal

In Thailand all the dishes are placed on the table at the same time. A typical meal consists of soup, a curry, a steamed dish, a fried dish, and a salad. These are served with one or two sauces or dips, and plain rice. Rice is the staple food of Thailand. Plain rice is served with a curry or soup; the more sophisticated rice dishes, such as Thai fried rice, are often served as an entrée.

Appetizers are a Western notion. In this section, we have presented a selection of dishes which could be served as starters. Desserts are usually only served at Thai banquets and on special occasions, but a number of sweet dishes are sold by street vendors as snacks.

Traditionally, a Thai meal is served at a low table. The diners sit round it on pillows. Each guest is given a plate, a fork, and a spoon and if soup is to be served, a small bowl and a ceramic Chinese-style spoon are also provided. Each diner helps himself or herself to a serving of rice. They then take a small amount of one dish, and after eating this they then move on to another dish. Generally speaking, Thais do not mix dishes on the plate. The dishes are eaten in any order. Thais eat from the spoon and generally only use the fork to mix the dish with rice and to push the food onto the spoon. Of course, how you serve the meal is entirely your choice, as the enjoyment of the food is the most important thing.

The easy, relaxed manner of eating Thai-style makes it the perfect cuisine for informal entertaining, and indeed, in Thailand, eating alone is considered one of life's great misfortunes. So armed with this book and a few essential ingredients, why not invite a few friends round to discover the joys of Thai cuisine.

The Ingredients

Don't be put off trying Thai cookery by the unusual ingredients used. When you look in the stores and supermarkets, you will be surprised just how many are readily available. As Thai food becomes more popular even convenience stores are stocking such delights as coconut milk, red and green curry paste, ginger root, and straw mushrooms. An Oriental food store is the best place to find the more unusual ingredients. Others can be substituted or sometimes left out altogether, but of course the finished dish becomes less authentic.

The following list of main ingredients used in Thai cuisine will make it easier to find them in the store and in addition, gives guidance on suitable substitutes.

Basil – Several varieties of basil are used in Thailand. Use the oriental variety if you can find it, or substitute home-grown basil for a different but equally delicious flavor. When adding basil to a dish it is best to tear the leaves rather than cut them as this releases more flavor.

Baby Eggplants – A number of different varieties of small, round eggplants are used in Thailand.

Unfortunately these are difficult to find in the West. You may be able to find baby white or green eggplants in Oriental food stores. If unavailable, substitute the standard purple eggplant cut into chunks.

Banana Leaves – These large leaves are used for wrapping food before steaming or baking. They impart a delicate flavor (and sometimes color) to the food which is cooked in them. Before use, wash the leaves well and soften, if necessary, by dipping in boiling water. The leaves are available fresh, usually folded up in large plastic bags, in the refrigerated sections of some Thai grocers. If unavailable, wrap food in nonstick baking paper or aluminum foil. Banana leaves are also cut into decorative shapes and used as a garnish (see Garnishes).

Bok Choy – This variety of Chinese or Nappa cabbage has stout white stems and bright green leaves, both of which are eaten. The delicate flavor lends itself to a variety of cooking methods, including stir-frying, braising, and steaming. It is sometimes available in large supermarkets as well as Oriental food stores, but if unavailable, substitute ordinary Chinese or Nappa cabbage.

Chilies – Chilies provide the heat in Thai dishes. The type most commonly used in Thai cooking are called "Birds Eye" chilies and are only ½-inch long. If you can't find them, use the Mexican chile pequin. Green chilies are hotter than red chilies of the same size and generally speaking, the smaller the chili the hotter it is. Jars or cans of ready-chopped chilies are very convenient for Thai cookery, or you can use whole dried and crushed chilies.

Coriander (cilantro) – Fresh coriander, also known as cilantro or Chinese parsley is used in many Asian cuisines, and, of course, in Mexican cooking. In Thailand, the root and stem are also used, particularly to flavor curries. Unfortunately coriander (cilantro) is usually trimmed of its roots. Use the roots if you can get them and the chopped stems. The leaves are often used whole or chopped, scattered over the top of dishes. Coriander (cilantro) seeds are also used as a spice.

Coconut and Coconut Milk – Coconut is an important ingredient in Thai food. It is most frequently used in the form of coconut milk. This is not to be confused with coconut water, which is the liquid inside the coconut. Coconut milk is made from the shredded meat of the coconut. You can buy canned coconut milk and coconut milk in a solid block called creamed coconut, as well as instant powdered coconut milk in many supermarkets. Thick and thin coconut milk and creamed coconut are used in Thai recipes. Canned coconut milk will yield all the different thicknesses of milk, because it separates into layers in the can. The top layer, the cream, is very thick and can be scooped away, leaving the thin milk underneath. To obtain thick milk, the contents of the can merely needs to be stirred together. Open cans will only keep 1 or 2 days in the refrigerator, but coconut milk freezes well so this is the best way to store any surplus. Instant powdered coconut milk is also fairly easy to find in supermarkets. Make this up as directed on the packet, or dissolve a block of creamed coconut in water to make the milk. You can even make milk from unsweetened fresh or dried shredded coconut. Always use unsweetened canned or shredded coconut (see Cooking Techniques).

Curry Paste – A glance through the recipes will show you that red and green curry pastes are used frequently. Green curry paste is the hotter of the two. Chilies and spices are pounded with a pestle in a mortar to form a paste. You may be able to get the paste ready-made from supermarkets or Oriental food stores. These are very convenient and avoid the need for the time-consuming pounding of all the ingredients. However, home-made curry pastes have a superior flavor so recipes are included in the Pastes and Dipping Sauces section of this book. A spice-grinder or electric coffee-grinder can help take the hard work out of preparation. For dishes with an Indian influence yellow curry paste is used – its color comes from the turmeric used in the mix. Curry pastes keep well; you can make double the quantity you need for a recipe and store it for later use. Keep refrigerated in airtight glass jars.

Dried Shrimp – These tiny shrimp are boiled and then sun-dried. They are stored in airtight glass jars as they have a very pungent smell. Used extensively in Thai cooking, they are available in Oriental food stores.

Fish Sauce – Fish sauce is used like soy sauce in Chinese cooking. Added to most dishes it eliminates the need to add salt. Use Thai or Vietnamese varieties. If unavailable, make your own (see Cooking Techniques).

Five-Spice Powder – A blend of powdered spices made from star anise, cassia bark, Sichuan peppercorns, cloves, and fennel seeds. It is available from most supermarkets as well as Oriental food stores. It is often known as Chinese five-spice powder.

Galangal (greater galangal or galingale) – A cousin of ginger, similar in appearance but with a milder, more fragrant flavor. Use it in the same way as ginger;

it is available fresh or dried from Oriental food stores. The dried version is known as Laos powder (the fresh root version is sometimes known by this name as well). If unavailable, substitute ginger which will give a slightly different flavor or omit altogether from the recipe.

Garlic – Used extensively as an ingredient in Thai cooking, fresh garlic is also chopped and fried until golden and used as a garnish. Although the garlic found in Thailand is smaller and milder than our own, ordinary garlic works just as well.

Garlic Chives – These are flat green chives with a very strong flavor and aroma. Substitute ordinary chives or the tops of green onions (scallions), and add a little extra garlic to the dish. Garlic chives are used in the classic noodle dish Pad Thai.

Ginger – Ginger is available fresh, dried, ground, and candied. Fresh root ginger is used in many dishes (see Cooking Techniques). When root ginger is added to a recipe it is usually chopped, although a slice is sometimes added to give a subtle flavor and then removed before serving.

Green Papaya – Like mango, papaya is eaten ripe as a dessert, or unripe as a savory ingredient. Use larger unripe green papayas found in Mexican and Oriental food stores to make the deliciously refreshing Green Papaya Salad.

Jasmine Water – This is used in Thai cooking in the same way as rosewater or orange flower water is used in the other cuisines. If you cannot find it, use kewra (orris root or screwpine) water or rosewater.

Kaffir Lime Leaves – These shiny, dark green leaves with a distinctive figure-of-eight-shape are an important flavoring in authentic Thai cooking. Used in a similar way to bayleaves they can be added whole or torn in half to add flavor to the dish, or shredded and used as a

garnish. They are available fresh, frozen, or dried. Dried lime leaves add very little flavor to the dish and are best avoided. Shredded lime rind can be substituted but the flavor will not be quite as authentic.

Lemongrass – Lemongrass imparts a delicious lemony tang to dishes and although lemon rind or juice can be substituted, the resulting flavor is not quite the same. Lemongrass is a herb with a fibrous texture, so is either bruised and used to infuse a dish with its flavor (in the same way as a bayleaf) or sliced very finely (see Cooking Techniques). It is also pounded into curry pastes. Avoid dried lemongrass as it has little flavor or aroma. Fresh lemongrass freezes well and is often available in larger supermarkets as well as most Oriental food stores. When you find it, trim away the outer leaves and freeze for future use.

Limes – Fresh lime juice is a basic ingredient and the fruit is often used for a garnish. Lemon can be substituted if limes are unavailable.

Long Beans – As the name suggests, these beans can grow to a length of about 2 feet. They are similar in flavor to wax or green beans, which can be used as a substitute if long beans are unavailable.

Noodles – A noodle dish is served at almost every Thai meal. Many types of noodle are eaten in Thailand but the most important are rice, cellophane, and egg noodles. Rice noodles are available dried in various sizes. Cellophane or glass noodles are made from mung beans; they are almost transparent in appearance. Egg noodles are wheat flour noodles. They are available both fresh and dried in this country and again come in various widths. They are used in soups and stir-fried dishes.

Palm Sugar – A thick brown sugar made from the boiled sap of the Palmyra palm or coconut palm. It is almost wet in texture and is available in tubs or cans from Oriental stores. Substitute an unrefined sugar such as light or dark raw brown sugar if it is unavailable.

Shrimp – For Thai dishes, try and use uncooked jumbo shrimp. These are sometimes available frozen. If you are unable to get them, use cooked shrimp, but add them at the last moment, reducing the heat and cooking just long enough to heat them through. Overcooking will make shrimp tough.

Rice – No Thai meal is complete without a rice dish. Three main types of rice are used. Jasmine, also known as Thai fragrant rice, is world-renowned. It is also the most popular rice used in Thailand.  This long-grained, fluffy white rice has a distinctive but subtle flavor which will be destroyed if salt is added during the cooking. Sticky or glutinous rice is a short-grained rice which becomes very sticky when cooked. It is popular in the north and northeast, where it is used to accompany savory dishes. Elsewhere, it is used for sweet dishes. Black glutinous rice is a dark, short-grained rice mainly used in desserts.

Salted Black Beans – These are fermented, salted soybeans. The beans are sold in little plastic bags and will keep for a long time if transferred to an airtight glass jar. Rinse and drain the beans well prior to using and crush or chop them before adding to a dish. If you cannot find them, used Chinese black bean sauce.

Shallots – The Thai shallot is used extensively in cooking; it has an attractive purplish-pink tinge and a strong flavor. Any type of shallot will do instead or use a little chopped onion.

Shrimp Paste – Also known as blachen and available in jars or in blocks, this paste is used to add flavor and saltiness to many Thai dishes. It has a very pungent smell so should be stored in an airtight glass jar. Shrimp paste must be fried before use – this is usually stated in the recipe instructions.

Soy Sauce – Used as a seasoning in some Thai dishes. Use light or dark soy as you prefer. Light soy sauce is sweeter and saltier than the dark soy sauce.

Green Onions (scallions) – Often used as a garnish (see Garnishes) and sometimes to impart their mild onion flavor to a dish.

Spring Roll Wrappers – These sheets of dough are sold frozen and must not be refrozen once thawed. Keep well wrapped during use, or they will dry out and crack. If unavailable, use sheets of strudel or phyllo dough from continental delis.

Star Anise – These star-shaped seed pods have a licorice flavour. They are available whole or ground. Fennel seeds can be substituted.

Straw Mushrooms – Available in cans from Oriental stores and supermarkets. Substitute fresh store mushrooms or oyster mushrooms if unavailable.

Tamarind – Made from the ripe pods of the tamarind tree. The reddish-brown pulp is sold in blocks; the juice is extracted and used in fish and meat dishes (see Cooking Techniques). If unavailable use lemon juice.

Turmeric – Adds a bright yellow color to many dishes, especially those of Indian or moslem origin.

Won ton Wrappers – Also known as won ton skins, these are made from an egg noodle dough which is rolled out until wafer thin and cut into squares. Like spring roll wrappers, they should be kept covered during use to prevent them from drying out.

Chapter 1
Soups
&
Appetizers

Curry Parcels • Glass Noodle Soup • Thai Omelet
Rice Soup with Pork • Thai Spring Rolls • Beef Saté
Coconut Shrimp Soup • Son-in-law Eggs
Pork Wrapped in Noodles • Beef Noodle Soup
Mussels in Chili Sauce • Thai Pork Stuffed Omelets
Spicy Shrimp Wraps • Chicken Coconut Soup

CURRY PARCELS

A tasty snack which can be served
as an appetizer.

MAKES 18

8 ounces chicken breast meat
2 tbsps oil
1 small onion, minced
2 cups diced, cooked potato
1 tbsp Red or Green Curry Paste (see Pastes
   and Dipping Sauces)
2 tsps sugar
18 won ton wrappers
Oil for deep-frying
Cucumber slices, to garnish

1. Skin the chicken and chop finely. Heat the oil in a wok and stir-fry the onion and chicken for 3 minutes.

2. Stir in the potato, curry paste, and sugar and fry for a few minutes. Remove the chicken mixture to a plate.

3. Place the won ton wrappers in front of you on a damp cloth to prevent them drying out too quickly. Spoon a little of the filling into the center of one of the wrappers.

4. Dampen the edges with water. Pull up the edges of the pastry and pinch together, enclosing the filling. Repeat until you have used up all the filling.

5. Heat the oil for deep-frying in a clean wok and deep-fry a few parcels at a time for 3-4 minutes, or until crisp and golden.

6. Drain on kitchen paper, and garnish with cucumber slices.

Step 4 Dampen the edges with water, pull up the edges of the pastry and pinch together to enclose the filling.

Step 3 Place the won ton wrappers on a tea-towel and spoon a little of the filling onto the center of each wrapper.

Step 5 Deep-fry a few parcels at a time for 3-4 minutes or until crisp and golden.

Cook's Notes

Time
Preparation takes 20 minutes and cooking takes 30 minutes.

Serving Idea
Serve with Sweet and Sour Dipping Sauce.

GLASS NOODLE SOUP

This attractive soup contains spicy meatballs and, of course,
the cellophane noodles which give the dish its name.

SERVES 4

2 tbsps oil
2 cloves garlic, thinly sliced
2 ounces dried cellophane noodles
8 ounces skinned and boned chicken breast
2 tbsps Green Curry Paste (see Pastes and Dipping
   Sauces)
2 tbsps fish sauce
3 tbsps cornstarch
1 tbsp chopped coriander (cilantro) leaves
4 cups chicken broth
3 cups shredded bok choy
4 green onions (scallions), cut into 1-inch pieces

1. Heat the oil in a small skillet or wok and fry the garlic
until golden. Remove with a slotted spoon and drain on
kitchen paper.

2. Place the noodles in a large bowl and cover with hot
water, allow to soak until softened, then drain.

3. Cut the chicken into chunks, then place in a food
processor with the curry paste, fish sauce, cornstarch
and coriander (cilantro) and process until very finely
ground.

4. Remove the mixture from the processor and shape
into small balls.

5. Heat the broth in a large saucepan until boiling and
add the meatballs. Cook for 10-15 minutes, or until they
rise to the surface.

6. Add the softened noodles, bok choy and green
onions (scallions) and continue to cook for 5 minutes.
Serve sprinkled with the fried garlic slices.

Step 3 Place the chicken, curry paste, fish sauce, cornstarch and coriander (cilantro) into a food processor and process until very finely ground.

Step 4 Shape the mixture into small balls.

Step 5 Cook the meatballs for 10-15 minutes, or until they rise to the surface.

Cook's Notes

Time
Preparation takes 15 minutes
and cooking takes 15-20 minutes.

Variation
Use other types of noodles.

THAI OMELET

In Thailand, omelets are always presented with a hot dipping sauce.
SERVES 4

6 eggs
2 tbsps fish sauce
1 tsp water
1 small red chili, sliced
3 green onions (scallions), sliced
2 tbsps oil
Banana leaves and chili curls, to garnish

1. Place the eggs in a mixing bowl with the fish sauce and water, and whisk until well combined and slightly foaming. Stir in the chili and green onions (scallions).

2. Heat the oil in a heavy-based skillet and when a haze rises from the pan, add the egg mixture.

3. Reduce the heat and cook the egg mixture, by pulling the egg from the side of the pan as it sets, and letting

Step 1 Place the eggs in a mixing bowl with the fish sauce and water, and whisk until well combined and slightly frothy.

Step 1 Stir in the chilies and green onions (scallions).

Step 3 Cook the egg mixture by pulling the egg from the side of the pan as it sets, and letting the uncooked mixture run underneath.

the uncooked mixture run to the edges of the pan.

4. When the egg mixture is almost set, place the pan under a preheated broiler to brown the top.

5. Slide the omelet onto a serving plate and cut into wedges. Garnish with shapes cut from a banana leaf and chili curls. Serve with a dipping sauce.

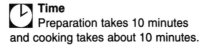

Cook's Notes

Time
Preparation takes 10 minutes and cooking takes about 10 minutes.

Serving Idea
Serve as a quick lunch dish for 2.

RICE SOUP WITH PORK
(KHAO TOM MOO)

This dish is often served for breakfast. Sometimes a
lightly-poached egg is added at the last moment.

SERVES 4

2 tbsps oil
2 cloves garlic, chopped
3½ cups pork or chicken broth
1 cup ground pork
3 cups cooked rice
2 sticks celery, sliced
2 green onions (scallions), sliced
1 tbsp chopped coriander (cilantro), leaves
   and stem
1 tbsp fish sauce
Pinch of white pepper

Step 2 Add the pork,
rice, celery and green
onions (scallions) to
the boiling broth and
simmer gently for 15
minutes.

Step 3 Stir in the
coriander (cilantro),
fish sauce and
pepper.

Step 1 Heat the oil in
small skillet or wok
and sauté the garlic
until pale golden.

1. Heat the oil in a small skillet or wok and fry the garlic
until pale golden. Remove with a slotted spoon and
drain on kitchen paper.

2. Bring the broth to the boil in a large saucepan. Add
the pork, rice, celery, and green onions (scallions) to
the pan and simmer gently for 15 minutes.

3. Stir in the coriander (cilantro), fish sauce, and
pepper. Serve sprinkled with the fried garlic.

Cook's Notes

Time
Preparation takes 10 minutes
and cooking takes about 20 minutes.

Variation
Use chicken instead of pork and
chop finely by hand or grind in a food
processor.

Cook's Tip
Cooked rice freezes very well,
and can be quickly reheated in boiling
water, or by microwaving or steaming.

THAI SPRING ROLLS (PO PIA TAUD)

Spring rolls have become so popular that they are now available in almost any supermarket. However, they are simple to make at home and will taste much better than the supermarket version.

MAKES ABOUT 12

2 tbsps oil
1 clove garlic, crushed
½ cup chopped pork
2 carrots, cut into thin sticks
2 sticks celery, cut into thin sticks
1 red or green chili, chopped
4 green onions (scallions), sliced
1 tsp grated fresh root ginger
1 tbsp chopped fresh coriander (cilantro)
1 tsp fish sauce
2 ounces cooked egg noodles
12 spring roll wrappers
Oil for deep-frying
Fresh coriander (cilantro) leaves, to garnish

1. Heat the oil in a wok or skillet and fry the garlic, pork, carrots, celery, and chili a few minutes until the pork is cooked and the vegetables are beginning to soften.

2. Stir in the green onions (scallions), ginger, coriander (cilantro), fish sauce, and noodles; cook gently to heat through.

Step 2 Stir the green onions (scallions), ginger, coriander (cilantro), fish sauce, and noodles into the wok and heat through.

3. Place a spring roll wrapper on a work surface and position a small amount of the filling across one corner. Roll up, folding in the corners to completely enclose the filling. Fill one spring roll at a time, keeping the remaining wrappers covered with a damp cloth to prevent them from drying out.

4. Just before serving, deep-fry the spring rolls in batches for 3-4 minutes or until crisp and golden. Garnish with fresh coriander (cilantro) and serve immediately.

Step 3 Place some filling across one corner of a spring roll wrapper and fold the corners over to completely enclose the filling.

Step 4 Deep-fry the spring rolls for 3-4 minutes or until crisp and golden.

Cook's Notes

Time
Preparation takes 20 minutes and cooking takes 20 minutes.

Serving Idea
Serve with Sweet Chili Sauce (see Pastes and Dipping Sauces).

Variation
Add chopped shrimp or bean sprouts to the filling.

BEEF SATÉ (NUEA SATAY)

A very popular Thai dish which can also be served as a light snack or as party food.

SERVES 4

8 ounces sirloin or fillet steak
Grated rind and juice of 1 lime
1 tsp chopped fresh chili
1 tbsp chopped fresh coriander (cilantro)
½ tsp ground turmeric
½ tsp ground cumin
2 tsps fish sauce
Oil for brushing
Chili "flowers" and green onion (scallion) "brushes,"
    to garnish

Saté Sauce

3 tbsps unsalted roasted peanuts
1 small red chili
Juice of 1 lime
¼ tsp ground cumin
¼ tsp ground coriander (cilantro)
2 tbsps thick coconut milk
2 tbsps oil
1 small onion, finely chopped
1 tbsp fish sauce
2-4 tbsps water

Step 1 Thread the beef strips onto bamboo skewers.

Step 2 Pour the marinade over the beef and leave for at least 1 hour.

1. Slice the steak thinly and thread pieces onto bamboo skewers. Place in a shallow dish.

2. Combine the lime rind and juice, chili, coriander (cilantro), turmeric, cumin, and fish sauce, and pour this over the beef. Turn the meat to coat it in the marinade and leave at least 1 hour, turning again once or twice.

3. To make the sauce, grind the peanuts, chili, lime juice, spices, and coconut milk in a pestle and mortar or food processor.

4. Heat the oil in a saucepan and sauté the onion until soft. Add the peanut mixture, the fish sauce, the beef marinade, and 2 tbsps water. Cook for 5 minutes.

5. Brush the satés with oil and barbecue or cook under a preheated broiler 3-5 minutes or until cooked through. Serve with the saté sauce. Garnish with the chili and green onions.

Cook's Notes

Time
Preparation takes 15 minutes, plus 1 hour marinating. Cooking takes 10 minutes.

Variation
Crunchy peanut butter can be used instead of ground peanuts.

Preparation
To make it easier to slice the steak thinly, partially freeze the meat. Cut across the grain to keep the meat tender.

COCONUT SHRIMP SOUP

Soup is usually served as part of a full Thai meal, but is also
eaten at any time as a snack or entrée on its own.

SERVES 4

1 stem lemongrass
4 raw jumbo shrimp
5 cups fish broth
4 slices galangal
4 kaffir lime leaves, shredded
2 red or green chilies, chopped
1 tbsp fish sauce
8 ounces skinned white fish fillets, cut into strips
⅔ cup thick coconut milk

1. Thinly slice a piece of the lemongrass about 2 inches long.

2. Peel the jumbo shrimp, leaving just the tails.

3. Pull the dark vein from the tails and discard it.

4. Heat the broth in a large saucepan until almost boiling and stir in the galangal, lime leaves, lemongrass, chilies, and fish sauce. Simmer for 2 minutes.

5. Add the fish strips and shrimp and cook gently for 5 minutes.

Step 2 Peel the jumbo shrimp, leaving just the tails.

Step 3 Pull away the dark vein from the shrimp tails.

6. Stir the coconut milk into the mixture and continue cooking until very hot, but do not allow to boil.

Cook's Notes

Time
Preparation takes 20 minutes and cooking takes 10 minutes.

Cook's Tip
Use a firm-fleshed fish that won't break up too much during cooking.

Variation
Ginger root can be used instead of galangal.

SON-IN-LAW EGGS
(KAI LEUK KOEY)

This popular and well-known Thai dish is traditionally made with duck eggs but chicken's eggs can be used instead.

SERVES 4

Sauce
⅔ cup tamarind juice
3 tbsps dark brown sugar
6 tbsps fish sauce

Oil for deep-frying
4 shallots, thinly sliced
4 cloves garlic, thinly sliced
4 hard-cooked eggs, peeled
Green onion (scallion) "brushes" and chili "flowers,"
  to garnish

1. Combine the sauce ingredients in a small saucepan and heat gently, stirring until the sugar dissolves. Bring to the boil, then reduce the heat and simmer gently for 5-10 minutes.

2. Heat the oil to 350°F in a wok. Add the shallots and fry 1-2 minutes, until golden-brown and crisp. Remove with a skimmer and drain on kitchen paper.

3. Add the garlic and fry for 1 minute, until pale golden, taking care not to allow it to burn. Drain on kitchen paper.

4. Add the eggs to the wok and deep-fry 5-10 minutes, until golden and bubbly on all sides. Keep turning the eggs so that they do not burn underneath. When golden, remove from the oil and drain on kitchen paper.

Step 4 Add the eggs to the hot oil and deep-fry for 5-10 minutes. Keep turning the eggs so that they do not burn.

Step 5 Slice the eggs in half lengthwise and arrange on a serving platter. Sprinkle the fried shallots and garlic over them.

5. Slice the eggs in half lengthwise and arrange on a serving platter. Sprinkle the fried shallots and garlic over the egg. Serve the sauce in a separate bowl, or pour it over the eggs. Garnish with the green onion (scallion) "brushes" and chili "flowers."

Cook's Notes

Time
Preparation takes 20 minutes and cooking takes 15-20 minutes.

Watchpoint
Allow the oil to cool before discarding it from the wok.

PORK WRAPPED IN NOODLES

Relatively mild in flavor, these crisp bundles
are served with a hot dipping sauce.

SERVES 4

1 cup ground pork
1 tsp ground coriander (cilantro) seeds
1 tbsp fish sauce
1 small egg, beaten
3 ounces rice noodles, uncooked
Oil for deep-frying
Whole chilies, to garnish

Step 2 Cover the noodles with warm water and leave to soak for about 10 minutes to soften.

1. Mix together the pork, coriander (cilantro), and fish sauce, then add enough egg to bind. Roll the mixture into small balls and chill for 30 minutes.

2. Cover the noodles with warm water and soak for about 10 minutes to soften. Drain the noodles, then

Step 2 Drain the noodles then wrap several strands around each pork ball.

Step 1 Roll the pork mixture into small balls and chill for 30 minutes.

wrap several strands around each pork ball.

3. Heat the oil in a wok and deep-fry a few at a time for 3-4 minutes, or until crisp and golden. Drain on kitchen paper and garnish with whole chilies.

Cook's Notes

Time
Preparation takes 20 minutes, plus 30 minutes chilling time. Cooking takes about 20 minutes.

Serving Idea
Serve with a hot dipping sauce such as Nam Prik or Sweet Chili Sauce.

BEEF NOODLE SOUP

You can use any type of noodle in this recipe –
substitute rice or cellophane noodles for a change.

SERVES 4

2 tbsps oil
8 ounces fillet steak, cut into thin strips
1 small onion, chopped
2 sticks celery, sliced diagonally
6 cups chicken or beef broth
1 tbsp chopped coriander (cilantro) root and stem
2 kaffir lime leaves
1-inch piece fresh root ginger, peeled and
    thinly sliced
1 tsp palm sugar
1 tbsp fish sauce
3 ounces egg noodles, uncooked
½ cup canned straw mushrooms, drained
Chili "flowers," to garnish

1. Heat the oil in a wok or saucepan and fry the steak, onion, and celery until the meat is cooked through

Step 1 Fry the meat, onion, and celery in a wok until the meat is cooked through and the vegetables are soft.

Step 2 Add the broth, coriander (cilantro), lime leaves, ginger, sugar, and fish sauce to the wok and bring to the boil.

and the vegetables are soft.

2. Add the broth, coriander (cilantro), lime leaves, ginger, sugar, and fish sauce. Bring to the boil.

3. Add the noodles and straw mushrooms and cook 10 minutes. Serve piping hot, garnished with chili "flowers."

Step 3 Add the noodles and mushrooms, and cook for 10 minutes.

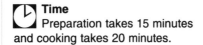

Cook's Notes

⏱ Time
Preparation takes 15 minutes and cooking takes 20 minutes.

👨‍🍳 Cook's Tip
Partially freeze the beef to make slicing easier. Cut the meat across the grain to keep it tender.

MUSSELS IN CHILI SAUCE

Seafood is an important part of the Thai diet.
Here mussels are served in a simple chili sauce.

SERVES 4

4 cups live mussels
1¼ cups water
1 stem lemongrass, chopped
1-inch piece fresh ginger root, peeled and sliced
4 dried kaffir lime leaves

Chili Sauce
3 large red chilies, chopped
4 tbsps chopped coriander (cilantro)
2 cloves garlic, crushed
2 tbsps oil
2 tbsps fish sauce
1 tbsp sugar
1 tbsp fresh basil, chopped
2 tsps cornstarch mixed with 2 tsps water

Basil leaves and chili "flowers," to garnish

1. Scrub the mussels and remove the beards, discarding any with broken shells, or those that do not close when tapped.

2. Bring the water to the boil, and add the lemongrass, ginger, and lime leaves. Add the mussels, cover and

Step 1 Scrub the mussels and remove the beards.

Step 2 Bring the water to the boil and add the lemongrass, ginger, and lime leaves.

cook 5-6 minutes or until the shells open.

3. Drain, reserving ⅔ cup of the cooking liquid. Discard any mussels that have not opened.

4. While the mussels are cooking, start to prepare the sauce. Pound the chilies, coriander (cilantro), and garlic together in a pestle and mortar.

5. Heat the oil in a wok and sauté the chili mixture for a few minutes, then stir in the fish sauce, sugar, and basil.

6. Add the reserved cooking liquid from the mussels and the dissolved cornstarch. Cook until slightly thickened.

7. Pour the sauce over the mussels before serving. Garnish with basil leaves and chili "flowers."

Step 5 Fry the chili mixture for a few minutes.

Cook's Notes

Time
Preparation takes 10 minutes and cooking takes 10-12 minutes.

Watchpoint
Do not overcook the mussels as they will become tough. Remove from the heat as soon as they open.

THAI PORK STUFFED OMELETS
(KAI YAHT SAI)

Plain omelets filled with a spicy pork mixture make a delicious
starter or snack. Serve with a dipping sauce.

SERVES 2

Filling
2 tbsps oil
1 small green chili, sliced
1 clove garlic, crushed
2 shallots, chopped
⅔ cup ground pork
4 shrimp, peeled and chopped
2 tbsps fish sauce
1 large canned tomato, chopped
2 tsps sugar
Pinch of white pepper
2 tbsps chopped coriander (cilantro) leaves

Omelets
4 eggs
1 tbsp fish sauce
1 tsp water
2 tbsps oil

Chili "'flowers," to garnish

1. To make the filling, heat the oil and fry the chili, garlic, and shallots for 3 minutes or until softened.

2. Add the ground pork and cook until it has turned color, breaking it up with a fork as it cooks.

3. Add the remaining filling ingredients and stir-fry 3-4 minutes. Keep warm while cooking the omelets.

4. To make the omelets, whisk the eggs in a mixing bowl with the fish sauce and water, beating until well combined and slightly foaming.

5. Heat half the oil in a small heavy-based skillet and when hot, pour in half the egg mixture. Reduce the heat and cook, using a spatula to lift the egg from the sides of the pan and tipping the pan as it sets.

6. When the egg mixture is almost set, gently flip it over or place under a preheated broiler to brown the top. Spoon half the pork mixture into the center of the omelet and fold over to completely enclose the filling. Transfer to a serving platter to keep warm. Make and fill a second omelet with the remaining egg and pork mixture. Serve with a dipping sauce and garnish with chili "flowers."

Step 6 Spoon half the pork mixture into the center of the omelet.

Step 6 Fold the omelet up to completely enclose the filling.

Cook's Notes

🕐 **Time**
Preparation takes 15 minutes and cooking takes 20-25 minutes.

🍳 **Cook's Tip**
If you have two small skillets cook both omelets at once.

SPICY SHRIMP WRAPS

Use uncooked jumbo shrimp for this dish. If you can't get fresh ones, look out for them in the freezer cabinet in Oriental grocery stores and large supermarkets.

SERVES 4

12 raw shrimp
1 clove garlic, crushed
1 stem lemongrass, finely sliced
1 red chili, seeded and chopped
1 tsp grated fresh root ginger
Juice of 1 lime
12 small spring roll wrappers
Oil for deep-frying

Step 4 Turn the shrimp in the marinade to coat them. Refrigerate for 2 hours, turning occasionally.

Step 2 Cut through the back of each shrimp without slicing right through the body.

1. Peel the shrimp, removing their heads and body shells, but leaving the tail fins attached.

2. Remove the dark vein and "butterfly" the shrimp by making a deep cut through the back without slicing right through the bodies. Carefully open them out.

3. Combine the garlic, lemongrass, chili, ginger, and lime juice in a shallow dish, and add the shrimp.

4. Turn the shrimp so that they are coated in the marinade. Marinate in the refrigerator for 2 hours, turning occasionally.

5. Just before serving, remove the shrimp from the marinade, and wrap each in a spring roll wrapper, leaving the tail-ends showing.

6. Heat the oil to 350°F in a wok and fry the shrimp wraps in batches for 3-4 minutes, or until golden. Drain on kitchen paper.

Step 5 Remove the shrimp from the marinade and wrap each in a spring roll wrapper, leaving the tail-ends showing.

Cook's Notes

Time
Preparation takes 20 minutes, plus 2 hours marinating. Cooking takes about 12 minutes.

Serving Idea
Serve with a hot dipping sauce, such as Nuoc Cham.

CHICKEN COCONUT SOUP
(TOM KHA GAI)

This is a rich aromatic soup, and its mild flavor makes it particularly popular with those new to Thai food.

SERVES 4

1 chicken breast, skinned and boned
2 cups thick coconut milk
1 cup chicken broth
6 slices galangal
2 red chilies, seeded and cut into strips
6 black peppercorns, crushed
4 kaffir lime leaves, torn in half
1 stem lemongrass, bruised
4 tbsps fish sauce
4 tbsps lime juice

Step 2 Combine the coconut milk and chicken broth in a large saucepan and bring to the boil.

Step 1 Use a sharp knife to cut the chicken into thin strips across the grain.

3. Reduce the heat to a simmer and add the chicken, galangal, chilies, peppercorns, lime leaves, and lemongrass. Simmer gently for 15-20 minutes, or until the chicken is tender and cooked through.

4. Add the fish sauce and lime juice and serve.

Step 4 Add the fish sauce and lime juice then serve immediately.

1. Use a sharp knife to cut the chicken into thin strips across the grain.

2. Combine the coconut milk and chicken broth in a large saucepan and bring to the boil.

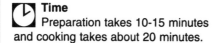
Cook's Notes

Time
Preparation takes 10-15 minutes and cooking takes about 20 minutes.

Cook's Tip
To make the chicken easier to slice, partially freeze it so that it holds its shape to allow thin and even strips to be cut.

Chapter 2

Fish & Seafood

Fried Spice Fish • Stir-fried Seafood

Sweet-and-sour Fish • Steamed Fish • Broiled Red Snapper

Shrimp in Green Curry Paste • Whole Steamed Fish in Yellow

Curry Sauce • Fish Cakes • Steamed Shrimp

Steamed Fish in Banana Leaves • Seafood with Egg Noodles

Fried Fish with Tamarind • Sweet Shrimp and Coconut Curry

FRIED SPICE FISH

In this recipe, a classic Thai sweet-and-sour chili sauce is poured over deep-fried fish.

SERVES 2-4

1 large whole fish, eg. red snapper, pomfret, or catfish,
  cleaned and scaled (if necessary)
3 tbsps cornstarch
1 tbsp sesame oil
3 large green chilies, seeded and chopped
1 tbsp grated fresh root ginger
2 cloves garlic, crushed
3 tbsps white wine vinegar
2 tbsps fish sauce
6 tbsps water
2 tbsps palm sugar
6 green onions (scallions), sliced
2 tbsps soy sauce
Oil for frying

1. Cut 3 or 4 slashes into each side of the fish. Dust with 2 tbsps of the cornstarch. Set aside.

2. Heat the sesame oil in a wok and stir-fry the chilies, ginger, and garlic for 2 minutes or until softened.

3. Add the vinegar, fish sauce, water, and sugar and simmer gently for 5 minutes. Stir in the green onions (scallions). Combine the remaining cornstarch and soy sauce and add to the pan; cook until slightly thickened. Keep warm.

Step 1 Cut 3-4 slashes into each side of the fish.

Step 1 Dust with 2 tbsps of the cornstarch.

4. Pour about 2 inches of oil into a wok or large sauté pan and heat. Fry the fish for 5-10 minutes or until cooked through. Place the fish on a serving platter and pour the sauce over it.

Cook's Notes

Time
Preparation takes 20 minutes and cooking takes about 20 minutes.

Preparation
The exact cooking time of the fish will depend on its thickness. The flesh should flake easily when it is cooked.

Variation
Small whole fish can be used instead, so each guest has their own.

STIR-FRIED SEAFOOD

Seafood plays a prominent part in Thai cooking, especially in the south.
SERVES 4

1 tsp black peppercorns
1 shallot, chopped
2 small red chilies, sliced
3 cloves garlic, crushed
2 tbsps oil
1½ cups peeled raw shrimp
2 cups prepared mixed seafood, eg. clams,
    squid, scallops
1 tbsp fish sauce
1 tbsp lime juice
4 green onions (scallions), sliced

1. Place the black peppercorns in a pestle and mortar and crush well. Add the shallot, chilies, and garlic and continue to pound until well combined.

Step 1 Crush the peppercorns in a pestle and mortar.

2. Heat the oil in a wok, add the chili mixture and stir-fry for 1 minute.

3. Add the shrimp and the rest of the seafood and stir-fry for 3-4 minutes, or until cooked through.

4. Sprinkle with fish sauce and lime juice. Serve scattered with green onion (scallion) slices.

Step 1 Add the shallot, chilies, and garlic, and continue pounding until well combined.

Step 2 Add the chili mixture to the oil in a wok, and stir-fry for 1 minute.

Cook's Notes

Time
Preparation takes 10 minutes and cooking takes 5-6 minutes.

Cook's Tip
Prepared mixed seafood can be bought in some large supermarkets.

SWEET-AND-SOUR FISH

In Thailand, fish is often fried in a wok and served
with a hot sauce, as with this recipe.

SERVES 2

2 whole white sea fish, each weighing
   1 pound, cleaned and scaled
6 tbsps oil
4 green chilies, seeded and sliced
1-inch piece fresh root ginger, peeled and cut
   into thin sticks
2 cloves garlic, crushed
1 carrot, peeled and cut into thin sticks
3 tbsps white wine vinegar
1 tbsp fish sauce
4 tbsps dark brown sugar
4 tbsps fish broth
6 green onions (scallions), shredded
1 tsp cornstarch mixed with 2 tsps water

Step 2 Fry the
chillies, garlic, ginger
and carrot for 3-4
minutes.

Step 4 Stir the
cornstarch and water
mixture into the wok
and cook until the
sauce thickens.

Step 1 Cut several
slashes in each side
of the fish.

1. Cut several slashes in each side of the fish. Heat
some oil in a wok or skillet and fry the fish for 5-10

minutes on each side. Remove from the pan and keep
warm while preparing the sauce.

2. Wipe out the pan and heat a little more oil in it. Fry
the chilies, ginger, garlic, and carrot for 3-4 minutes.

3. Stir in the vinegar, fish sauce, sugar, and broth and
bring to the boil. Add the green onions (scallions).

4. Stir the cornstarch mixture into the wok; cook until the
sauce thickens. Pour over the fish to serve.

Cook's Notes

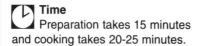

Time
Preparation takes 15 minutes
and cooking takes 20-25 minutes.

Variation
The fish can also be broiled or
barbecued.

STEAMED FISH

Steaming is a particularly suitable method of cooking fish as it does not mask or diminish the flavor. The ingredients added immediately after cooking give this dish that distinctive Thai touch.

SERVES 4

1 pound whitefish fillets, skinned
2 shallots, sliced
1 stem lemongrass, sliced
3 tbsps lime juice
2 tbsps fish sauce
1 tsp palm sugar
2 cloves garlic, chopped
1 red chili, chopped
1 green chili, chopped

1. Cut the fish into thick strips and place in a serving dish that will fit into the top of a steamer.

2. Scatter the sliced shallots and lemongrass over the fish and steam for 10 minutes or until the fish is cooked through.

3. Meanwhile, combine the lime juice, fish sauce, and sugar in a small bowl; stir until the sugar dissolves.

4. Combine the garlic and chilies together in another small bowl.

5. As soon as the fish is cooked, remove from the steamer and pour the fish sauce mixture over it. Scatter the chili-and-garlic mixture over the top and serve immediately.

Step 5 As soon as the fish is cooked, pour the fish sauce mixture over it.

Step 2 Scatter the sliced shallots and lemongrass over the fish.

Step 5 Scatter the chilli-and-garlic mixture over the top and serve immediately.

Cook's Notes

⏱ Time
Preparation takes 15 minutes and cooking takes about 10 minutes.

🔲 Cook's Tip
If wished, the seeds of the chilies can be removed for a milder flavor.

BROILED RED SNAPPER

Red snapper is a popular fish in Thailand and can be used for
many fish dishes. Sea bream, scrod, or redfish may be used if snapper is unavailable.

SERVES 2

1 large red snapper, cleaned and scaled
1 tbsp Green Curry Paste (see Pastes and
   Dipping Sauces)
⅔ cup thick coconut milk
3 tbsps fish sauce
2 tbsps palm sugar
3 lime leaves
2 stems lemongrass, sliced
Banana leaf, nonstick baking paper, or foil
Carrot and lemon " twigs," to garnish

1. Cut 3 or 4 slashes into each side of the fish, and place in a dish. Combine the remaining ingredients, except the banana leaf and garnish, and pour them over the fish. Allow to marinate for 1 hour.

2. Place the marinated fish on a piece of blanched banana leaf and pour some of the marinade over it. Wrap the fish in the banana leaf until completely enclosed and place in a flameproof dish. Use baking parchment or foil if banana leaves are unavailable.

3. Broil under medium heat for 25-30 minutes, turning halfway through cooking. Alternatively, bake in an oven

Step 1 Pour the marinade over the snapper and leave to stand for 1 hour.

Step 2 Place the marinated fish on a piece of banana leaf, pour over some of the marinade and wrap up.

preheated to 350°F, for 30 minutes.

4. Using scissors, cut a large cross in the banana leaf and serve the fish in the banana leaf, garnished with carrot and lemon "twigs."

Cook's Notes

Time
Preparation takes 10 minutes, plus 1 hour marinating. Cooking takes 25-30 minutes.

Buying Guide
Buy fish that has bright eyes and firm flesh.

SHRIMP IN GREEN CURRY PASTE

This is the hottest of Thai curries because of the large number
of small green chilies traditionally used in
the Green Curry Paste.

SERVES 2-3

1 cup thick coconut milk
2 tbsps Green Curry Paste (see Pastes and
   Dipping Sauces)
2 cups peeled, raw shrimp
1 tbsp fish sauce
Lemon rind, for garnish

Step 2 Gradually stir
in the remaining
coconut milk.

Step 1 Add the curry
paste to a little of the
coconut milk in a wok
and boil rapidly for 5
minutes, stirring
frequently.

1. Heat a little of the coconut milk in a wok and add the
curry paste. Boil rapidly for 5 minutes, stirring
frequently, then reduce the heat.

2. Gradually stir in the remaining coconut milk, then add
the shrimp and fish sauce. Cook gently for about 5
minutes or until shrimp are cooked. Garnish with lemon
rind and serve with steamed rice.

Cook's Notes

Time
Preparation takes 5 minutes and
cooking takes 10 minutes.

Serving Idea
Serve with Thai Steamed Rice.

WHOLE STEAMED FISH IN YELLOW CURRY SAUCE

Steaming is a very popular method of cooking in Thailand.
Here the fish is steamed in a delicious coconut curry sauce.

SERVES 2

2 red mullet, cleaned
1 tbsp oil
1 tbsp Yellow Curry Paste (see Pastes and
   Dipping Sauces)
1¼ cups thick coconut milk
2 tbsps fish sauce
2 tbsps light brown sugar
2 kaffir lime leaves

1. Cut 3 or 4 slashes on each side of the fish and place in a heatproof dish which will fit into the top of a steamer.

2. Heat the oil in a wok and fry the curry paste for 1-2 minutes. Stir in half the coconut milk and boil rapidly for 5 minutes.

3. Stir in the remaining coconut milk, fish sauce, sugar, and lime leaves.

4. Pour the sauce over the fish and steam for 15 minutes or until fish is cooked. Serve immediately.

Step 3 Stir the remaining coconut milk, fish sauce, sugar and lime leaves into the wok.

Step 4 Pour the sauce over the fish in a heat-proof dish.

Cook's Notes

Time
Preparation takes 15 minutes and cooking takes 25 minutes.

Preparation
The fish should flake easily when it is cooked.

FISH CAKES
(TAUD MAN PLA)

Fish cakes are just one of the delicious savories that
you can buy from street vendors in Bangkok,
where they make and cook them while you wait.

MAKES 8

10 ounces white fish fillets, skinned
3 tbsps Red Curry Paste (see Pastes and
   Dipping Sauces)
2 tbsps fish sauce
3 tbsps cornstarch
1 tbsp chopped coriander (cilantro) leaves
2 green onions (scallions), finely sliced
1 egg, beaten
Oil for frying
Carrot and green onion (scallion) strips, to garnish

the green onions (scallions) and enough egg to bind the
mixture together.

3. Dust your hands with flour and shape the mixture into
eight small rounds. Chill until required.

4. Shallow- or deep-fry for a few minutes on each side
until golden. Garnish with strips of carrot and green
onion (scallion).

Step 2 Beat in the
green onions
(scallions) and
enough egg to bind
the mixture together.

Step 1 Place the fish,
curry paste, fish
sauce, cornstarch,
and coriander
(cilantro) in a food
processor and
process until very
finely ground.

Step 3 Shape the
mixture into 8 small
cakes, using floured
hands.

1. Place the fish, curry paste, fish sauce, cornstarch,
and coriander (cilantro) in a food processor and
process until very finely ground.

2. Remove the mixture from the processor and beat in

Cook's Notes

Time
Preparation takes 10 minutes
and cooking takes 5 minutes.

Serving Idea
Serve with a dipping sauce or
Indian chutney.

STEAMED SHRIMP

Serve these simply-prepared shrimp with a rice dish such as
Shrimp Paste Fried Rice and a hot dipping sauce.

SERVES 2

1 pound raw shrimp, in the shell
2 tbsps sesame oil
2 cloves garlic, chopped
2 tbsps chopped fresh coriander (cilantro) root, stem
   and leaves
2 tsps grated fresh root ginger
1 red chili, sliced
1 green chili, sliced
2 tbsps soy sauce
Lemon and lime twists, to garnish

1. Wash and peel the shrimp.

2. Combine the remaining ingredients, except the garnish, in a small jug or bowl.

3. Place the shrimp in a heatproof bowl or plate that will fit into a steamer basket. Pour the sauce over

Step 2 Combine the sesame oil, garlic, coriander (cilantro), ginger, chilies, and soy in a small bowl.

Step 3 Pour the sauce over the shrimp in a heat-proof bowl.

Step 4 Place the bowl in a steamer; cover and steam for 15 minutes or until the shrimp are cooked through.

them and toss well.

4. Place the bowl in the steamer, cover and steam for 15 minutes or until the shrimp have turned pink and are cooked through.

5. Serve immediately, garnished with lemon and lime twists.

Cook's Notes

🕐 **Time**
Preparation takes 15 minutes and cooking takes about 15 minutes.

🍳 **Cook's Tip**
Do not overcook the shrimp or they will become tough.

STEAMED FISH IN BANANA LEAVES (HAW MOK)

Lining the steamer with banana leaves, as in Thailand, imparts extra flavor to the dish, but you can use nonstick baking paper or foil instead.

SERVES 4

1 pound whitefish fillets, skinned
Banana leaves (optional)
2 carrots, peeled and cut into thin sticks
1 red bell pepper, cut into strips
4 ounces long beans or green beans, cut into
　　3-inch lengths
2 zucchini, cut into thin sticks
⅔ cup thick coconut milk
1-2 tbsps Red Curry Paste (see Pastes and Dipping
　　Sauces)
2 kaffir lime leaves
1 tbsp fish sauce

1. Cut the fish into bite-sized pieces or strips about ½ inch wide.

2. Line a heatproof dish, which will fit into your steamer, with banana leaves, nonstick baking paper, or foil.

Step 1 Cut the fish into bite-size pieces or strips about ½-inch wide.

Step 2 Line a heatproof dish, which will fit into your steamer, with banana leaves.

Step 4 Pile the fish pieces on top of the vegetables in the steamer.

3. Blanch the carrots, bell pepper, and beans for 2 minutes in boiling water. Add the zucchini, cook 30 seconds then drain and scatter over the banana leaf.

4. Pile the fish on top of the vegetables.

5. Combine the remaining ingredients and pour them over the fish. Cover the steamer and steam for 15-20 minutes or until the fish is cooked through.

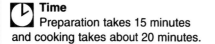

Cook's Notes

Time
Preparation takes 15 minutes and cooking takes about 20 minutes.

Cook's Tip
Use a firm-fleshed fish so that it won't fall to pieces during cooking.

SEAFOOD WITH EGG NOODLES

Use any mixture of seafood in this spicy dish, which can
be served as an entrée or an impressive side-dish.

SERVES 4

1 pound mixed fish and seafood, such as shrimp,
    chunks of whitefish, squid, clams, and mussels
3 large green chilies, seeded and chopped
1 tbsp chopped fresh coriander (cilantro) leaves
2 cloves garlic, crushed
6 ounces uncooked egg noodles
2 tbsps oil
1 cup snow peas
½ cup baby corn cobs
½ red pepper, sliced
1 tbsp fish sauce
⅔ cup fish broth
1 tbsp lime juice
2 tsps cornstarch

Step 2 Pound the chilies, coriander (cilantro) and garlic together in a pestle and mortar.

Step 4 Add the chili mixture and the fish sauce to the vegetables in the wok and cook for 2 minutes.

Step 1 If using squid, score the pouches in a diamond pattern before cutting into pieces.

1. Cook the seafood separately in boiling water until cooked through, then drain and set aside. If using squid, score the pouches in a diamond pattern before cutting into pieces.

2. Pound the chilies, coriander (cilantro), and garlic together in a pestle and mortar.

3. Cook the noodles as directed on the package.

4. Heat the oil in a wok, add the snow peas, baby corn, and pepper, and stir-fry for 4 minutes. Add the chili mixture and fish sauce and cook for 2 minutes.

5. Stir in the fish broth; add the cooked seafood and noodles to the pan. Mix the lime juice and cornstarch together. Stir into the wok and cook until thickened.

Cook's Notes

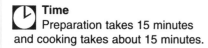 **Time**
Preparation takes 15 minutes and cooking takes about 15 minutes.

Cook's Tip
Scoring the squid helps to keep it tender during cooking.

 Buying Guide
Mixed prepared seafood can be bought from large supermarkets.

FRIED FISH WITH TAMARIND
(PLA TOD MAK HAM)

In this dish the fish is served with a delicious sweet and sour sauce.

SERVES 2-4

1 pound whole fish, eg. red snapper, sea bass, or
   yellowtail, cleaned
3 tbsps cornstarch
Oil for frying
2 cloves garlic, crushed
1 tbsp grated fresh root ginger
1 small red chili, sliced
1 small green chili, sliced
6 green onions (scallions), sliced
1 tbsp soy sauce
2 tbsps palm sugar
2 tbsps fish sauce
⅔ cup tamarind juice
Lemon twists, coriander (cilantro) leaves, and sliced
   green onion (scallion) tops, to garnish

1. Cut 2-3 slashes on each side of the fish and dredge
with the cornstarch.

2. Heat about 2 inches of oil in a wok and fry the fish
one at a time for about 5 minutes on each side. When
cooked, transfer to a serving platter and keep warm.

3. Carefully drain most of the oil from the wok and add
the garlic, ginger, chilies, and green onions (scallions);
stir-fry for 2-3 minutes.

4. Add the soy sauce, palm sugar, and fish sauce; stir

until the sugar dissolves.

5. Add the tamarind juice and heat though. Pour some
of the sauce over the fish and serve the remainder
separately. Garnish with lemon twists, coriander
(cilantro) leaves, and a pile of green onion (scallion)
slices.

Step 2 Fry the fish
one at a time for
about 5 minutes on
each side.

Step 3 Stir-fry the
garlic, ginger, chilies
and green onions
(scallions) for 2-3
minutes.

Cook's Notes

Time
Preparation takes 15 minutes
and cooking takes about 25 minutes.

Buying Guide
If using fish with large scales,
make sure they are scraped off before
cooking.

Preparation
The exact cooking time for the
fish will depend on its thickness. The
flesh will flake easily when it is
cooked.

SWEET SHRIMP AND COCONUT CURRY

This mild curry should be served with plain Thai Steamed Rice.

SERVES 4

3 cups raw shrimp, peeled
⅔ cup thick coconut milk
2 tsps lime juice
2 tbsps oil
1 clove garlic, crushed
4 shallots, sliced
1 tbsp grated fresh root ginger
1 tbsp Yellow Curry Paste (see Pastes and Dipping Sauces)
5 tsps palm sugar
Lemon and lime wedges and 1 tbsp toasted unsweetened shredded coconut, to garnish

1. Combine the shrimp, coconut milk, and lime juice in a shallow dish. Leave to marinate for at least 30 minutes, stirring occasionally.

2. Heat the oil in a wok and sauté the garlic and shallots until softened.

Step 1 Marinate the shrimp in the coconut milk and lime juice.

Step 3 Stir the ginger and curry paste into the wok and stir-fry for 1-2 minutes.

Step 4 Add the shrimp and their marinade to the wok and cook over a reduced heat for 5 minutes.

3. Stir in the ginger and curry paste and stir-fry for 1-2 minutes. Stir in the sugar.

4. Add the shrimp and their marinade to the wok and cook over a reduced heat for 5 minutes or until the shrimp turn pink.

5. Transfer to a serving dish and garnish with lemon and lime wedges. Sprinkle with the coconut and serve immediately.

Cook's Notes

Time
Preparation takes 10 minutes, plus at least 30 minutes marinating. Cooking takes about 10 minutes.

Buying Guide
Use bay shrimp or jumbo shrimp for this recipe.

Chapter 3

Meat & Poultry

Red Chicken Curry • Beef in Oyster Sauce
Spicy Ground Chicken • Pork Curry with Eggplant
Barbecued Chicken • Five-spice Pork • Baked Duck Salad
Green Curry with Beef • Stir-fried Chicken with Ginger
Steamed Pork Cups • Chicken and Peanut Curry
Spicy Ground Beef • Yellow Chicken Curry • Barbecued Pork
Chicken with Chili and Basil • Mussaman Curry

RED CHICKEN CURRY
(GAENG PED GAI)

Red and green curry pastes are the basis of most Thai curries
and this is a simple one flavored with red curry paste.

SERVES 4

1 pound chicken breasts, skinned and boned

2 tbsps oil

2 onions, peeled and cut into wedges

3 tbsps Red Curry Paste (see Pastes and Dipping
Sauces)

2 kaffir lime leaves, shredded

1¼ cups thick coconut milk

½ cup canned sliced bamboo shoots, drained

1 tbsp fish sauce

2 tbsps sugar

Step 2 Add the curry paste and lime leaves to the wok and fry for a few minutes.

2. Add the curry paste and lime leaves to the wok and fry for a few minutes. Stir in half of the coconut milk and boil rapidly for 3 minutes.

3. Return the chicken to the wok and add the bamboo shoots, fish sauce, and sugar. Simmer gently for 5 minutes or until the chicken is cooked. Stir in the remaining coconut milk and cook until heated through.

Step 1 Stir-fry the onion and chicken for 5 minutes or until the onion is softened and beginning to brown.

1. Cut the chicken into bite-sized pieces. Heat the oil in a wok and stir-fry the onion and chicken for 5 minutes or until the onion is softened and beginning to brown. Remove from the wok and set aside.

Step 3 Return the chicken to the wok then add the bamboo shoots, fish sauce and sugar. Simmer for 5 minutes or until the chicken is cooked.

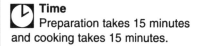

Cook's Notes

Time
Preparation takes 15 minutes and cooking takes 15 minutes.

Serving Idea
Accompany with Thai Steamed Rice and Cucumber Salad.

BEEF IN OYSTER SAUCE

You can make this spicy dish very quickly.

SERVES 4

1 pound sirloin steak
2 tbsps oil
¼ tsp ground cumin
¼ tsp ground coriander
1 cup baby sweetcorn
½ cup canned bamboo shoots, drained
1 cup snow peas
2 tbsps oyster sauce
2 tsps dark brown sugar
⅔ cup beef broth
1 tsp cornstarch
1 tbsp fish sauce
Green onion (scallion) slices, to garnish

1. Cut the beef into thin slices and then into strips, using a sharp knife.

2. Heat the oil in a wok and stir-fry the beef over a high

Step 1 Cut the beef into thin slices and then into strips.

Step 2 Fry the beef over a high heat for 5 minutes or until cooked through.

Step 4 Sprinkle with slices of green onion (scallion) to garnish.

heat for 5 minutes or until cooked through. Stir in the spices and cook for 1 minute.

3. Add the vegetables, then stir in the oyster sauce, sugar, and broth, and bring to the boil.

4. Mix the cornstarch with the fish sauce and stir into the pan, cooking until the sauce thickens. Sprinkle with slices of green onion (scallion) to garnish.

Cook's Notes

🕐 **Time**
Preparation takes 10 minutes and cooking takes 10 minutes.

🍳 **Cook's Tip**
Partially freezing the beef will make it easier to cut. Slice the meat into strips across the grain to keep it tender.

SPICY GROUND CHICKEN (LAAB KAI)

This version of a traditional Thai dish comes from northeastern Thailand, and contains glutinous rice which gives it a delicious, nutty flavor.

SERVES 4

2 tbsps glutinous rice
2 tbsps oil
2 cloves garlic, crushed
6 small red or green chilies, sliced
3 cups ground chicken
1 tbsp oyster sauce
1 tbsp fish sauce
1 tsp salted black beans
2 tbsps soy sauce
Green onion (scallion) slices, to garnish

1. Place the rice in a wok and dry-fry it for 5-10 minutes or until the grains are golden on all sides, shaking and stirring the wok as the rice cooks.

2. Pour the toasted rice into a pestle and mortar and pound until ground almost to a powder.

3. Heat the oil in the wok and fry the garlic and chilies for 2-3 minutes or until softened.

4. Add the chicken and stir-fry, breaking the chicken up as it cooks.

5. Once the chicken is cooked and no longer pink, stir in the oyster sauce, fish sauce, black beans, and soy sauce.

6. Add the ground rice and stir-fry for 2-3 minutes. Serve immediately, scattered with green onion (scallion) slices.

Step 1 Dry-fry the rice in a wok for 5-10 minutes or until the grains are golden on all sides.

Step 2 Grind the toasted rice in a pestle and mortar until almost a powder.

Step 6 Add the ground up rice to the ingredients in the wok and stir-fry for 2-3 minutes.

Cook's Notes

Time
Preparation takes 15 minutes and cooking takes 25-30 minutes.

Cook's Tip
If you don't have a pestle and mortar, put the rice into a plastic bag and crush with a rolling pin.

PORK CURRY WITH EGGPLANT

This hot and spicy pork curry can be served accompanied
with rice for a delicious meal in itself.

SERVES 6

2 pounds pork belly, sliced
2 tbsps oil
3 tbsps Red Curry Paste (see Pastes and Dipping
   Sauces)
2½ cups water
½ cup sliced bamboo shoots
6 small white eggplants, quartered
½ cup long beans, cut into 1-inch pieces
3 large green chilies, seeded and quartered
   lengthwise
2 tbsps fish sauce
1 tbsp lime juice
1 tsp palm sugar
Small bunch sweet basil, torn into pieces

2. Heat the oil in a wok and fry the curry paste for 2-3 minutes; add the meat and fry for 5 minutes.

3. Add the water and bring to the boil, then reduce the heat and add the bamboo shoots, eggplants, long beans, and chilies. Simmer gently for 10 minutes.

4. Stir in the fish sauce, lime juice, sugar, and basil and serve immediately.

Step 2 Add the pork to the curry paste in the wok and fry for 5 minutes.

Step 1 Cut the pork crosswise into 1-inch chunks.

1. Trim the rind from the pork if wished and cut the meat crosswise into 1-inch chunks.

Step 3 Add the bamboo shoots, eggplants, long beans, and chilies to the wok and simmer gently for 10 minutes.

Cook's Notes

Time
Preparation takes 20 minutes and cooking takes 25-30 minutes.

Cook's Tip
Make sure you add the basil at the last moment so that its flavor is preserved.

BARBECUED CHICKEN

These spicy chicken pieces are delicious served with a hot dipping sauce.

SERVES 4-6

1½ pounds chicken thighs
2 tbsps Red Curry Paste (see Pastes and Dipping Sauces)
2 cloves garlic, crushed
⅔ cup thick coconut milk
2 tbsps chopped coriander (cilantro) leaves, stem and root

Dipping Sauce
1 small red chili, sliced
1 small green chili, sliced
4 tbsps white wine vinegar

Banana leaves and chili halves, to garnish

1. Place the chicken pieces in a large mixing bowl.

2. Combine the curry paste, garlic, coconut milk, and coriander (cilantro) and pour over the chicken. Toss together until all the chicken pieces are well coated. Leave to marinate for 2 hours.

3. Combine the sliced chilies and vinegar to make the dipping sauce, and set aside until required.

4. Cook the chicken pieces over a preheated barbecue or under a preheated broiler for 10-15 minutes or until tender. Turn frequently and baste with any remaining marinade during cooking.

5. Serve the chicken hot or cold with the dipping sauce. Garnish with shapes cut from a banana leaf and chili halves.

Step 2 Combine the curry paste, garlic, coconut milk, and coriander (cilantro), and pour over the chicken in a large dish.

Step 2 Turn the chicken in the marinade and leave to stand for 2 hours.

Step 3 Combine the sliced chilies and vinegar in a small bowl and set aside until you are ready to serve the dish.

Cook's Notes

Time
Preparation takes 10 minutes, plus 2 hours marinating. Cooking takes 10-15 minutes.

Serving Idea
This dish is perfect accompanied with Thai Steamed Rice and Green Papaya Salad.

FIVE-SPICE PORK
(SEE-KRONG MOO OB)

Serve this delicious, sweet, spicy dish with rice.

SERVES 4

1½ pounds pork belly, sliced
2 tbsps oil
1 tbsp Red Curry Paste (see Pastes and Dipping
   Sauces)
2 tbsps fish sauce
1 tbsp light soy sauce
2 tbsps sugar
1 tsp five-spice powder
1 tbsp chopped lemongrass
Fresh coriander (cilantro) and lime twists, to garnish

Step 2 Stir the fish sauce, soy sauce, sugar, five-spice, and lemongrass into the curry paste in the wok. Cook for 3 minutes.

Step 1 Cut the pork strips crosswise into 1½-inch chunks.

spice powder and lemongrass. Cook 3 minutes.

3. Add the pork to the wok and cook, tossing frequently for 10 minutes or until the pork is cooked through.

4. Serve garnished with fresh coriander (cilantro) and lime twists.

Step 3 Add the pork to the ingredients in the wok and cook, tossing frequently, for 10 minutes.

1. Cut the pork strips into 1½-inch chunks.

2. Heat the oil in a wok and fry the curry paste for 2 minutes. Add the fish sauce, soy sauce, sugar, five-

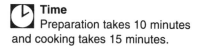

Cook's Notes

Time
Preparation takes 10 minutes and cooking takes 15 minutes.

Preparation
You can trim the rind from the pork if preferred.

BAKED DUCK SALAD

A refreshing salad which makes a delicious meal
in itself, served with steamed rice.

SERVES 4-6

4 duck breasts
1 tsp paprika
1 x 11oz can mandarin segments, in natural juice
2 tbsps white wine vinegar
2 tbsps oyster sauce
2 tbsps sesame oil
½ tsp dried chili flakes
½ cup flaked, unsweetened coconut
2 tbsps roasted cashew nuts
Flaked coconut, to garnish

1. Place the duck breasts on a trivet in a roasting pan and sprinkle with the paprika.

2. Roast in an oven preheated to 400°F, for 35-40 minutes, or until cooked. Allow to cool and cut into thin slices.

Step 1 Place the duck breasts on a trivet in a roasting pan, and sprinkle the skin with the paprika.

Step 3 Drain the juice from the mandarins and combine the vinegar, oyster sauce, oil and chili flakes.

Step 3 Pour the sauce over the cooked duck and leave to marinate for at least 3 hours.

3. Drain the mandarins and reserve the juice. Combine the juice with the vinegar, oyster sauce, oil, and chili flakes. Pour this sauce over the sliced duck and leave to marinate for at least 3 hours.

4. Just before serving, sprinkle the coconut and cashew nuts over the duck. Transfer to a serving platter and arrange the mandarin segments in the center. Serve garnished with a little extra flaked coconut.

Cook's Notes

Time
Preparation takes 20 minutes plus at least 3 hours marinating time. Cooking takes 40 minutes.

Buying Guide
Duck breasts are now available at most large supermarkets.

GREEN CURRY WITH BEEF

Serve this popular Thai curry with rice.

SERVES 4

2 tbsps oil

3 tbsps Green Curry Paste (see Pastes and Dipping Sauces)

12 ounces sirloin or rump steak, sliced

2 cups thick coconut milk

2 tbsps fish sauce

4 kaffir lime leaves, torn in half

8 small white eggplants, quartered

2 large red chilies, quartered lengthwise

1-inch piece galangal, sliced

1 tsp palm sugar

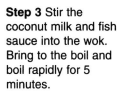

Step 3 Stir the coconut milk and fish sauce into the wok. Bring to the boil and boil rapidly for 5 minutes.

Step 4 Add the lime leaves, eggplants, chilies, galangal and sugar to the wok. Simmer for 5-10 minutes.

Step 2 Add the sliced beef to the curry paste in the wok and stir-fry for 2 minutes or until the meat turns color.

1. Heat the oil in a wok, add the curry paste, and fry for 2 minutes, stirring frequently.

2. Add the beef slices and stir-fry for 2 minutes or until the meat turns color.

3. Stir in the coconut milk and fish sauce and bring to the boil. Boil rapidly for 5 minutes, stirring occasionally.

4. Reduce the heat and stir in the lime leaves, eggplants, chilies, galangal and sugar. Simmer for 5-10 minutes or until the eggplants are tender.

Cook's Notes

Time
Preparation takes 15 minutes and cooking takes 20 minutes.

Cook's Tip
Partially freeze the beef to make cutting easier, and slice the meat across the grain to keep it tender.

STIR-FRIED CHICKEN WITH GINGER

This dish appears on many Thai restaurant menus.
It can be served with either rice or noodles.

SERVES 4

2 tbsps oil
2 cloves garlic, crushed
2 shallots, chopped
12 ounces chicken breast, skinned, boned and cut
    into thin strips
2-inch piece fresh root ginger, peeled and cut
    into sticks
2 kaffir lime leaves, shredded
2 tbsps whole blanched almonds
1 cup long beans, cut into 2-inch lengths
1 red bell pepper, cut into strips
½ cup water chestnuts, sliced
3 tbsps fish sauce
1 tbsp sugar

1. Heat the oil in a wok and fry the garlic and shallots until beginning to soften. Add the chicken strips and stir-fry until they change colour.

2. Add the ginger, lime leaves, almonds, beans, pepper and water chestnuts.

3. Stir-fry, tossing the ingredients frequently, for 5 minutes or until vegetables are cooked but still crisp. Stir in the fish sauce and sugar and serve.

Step 2 Add the ginger, lime leaves, almonds, beans, bell pepper, and water chestnuts to the wok. Stir-fry 5 minutes or until the vegetables are tender and crisp.

Step 1 Fry the garlic and shallots until beginning to soften.

Step 3 Stir the fish sauce and sugar into the wok.

Cook's Notes

Time
Preparation takes 15 minutes and cooking takes 10 minutes.

Variation
Use unsalted roasted cashew nuts in place of the almonds.

Preparation
Cut the chicken across the grain to keep it tender.

STEAMED PORK CUPS

Served with a light salad and accompanied with a hot dipping sauce
this spicy pork mixture makes an ideal luncheon dish.

SERVES 4-6

1 pound boneless lean pork
5 cloves garlic, crushed
6 green onions (scallions), sliced
2 green chilies, sliced
1 tbsp roasted cashew nuts
1 tsp shrimp paste
2 tbsps soy sauce
2 tbsps coriander (cilantro) leaves and stem
Pinch of white pepper
1 tsp palm sugar
½ cup thick coconut milk
2 egg whites

Salad
1 red pepper, sliced
1 green pepper, sliced
2 cups bean sprouts
2 tbsps lime juice
1 tbsp fish sauce

Step 3 Fold the beaten egg white into the pork mixture using a spatula.

Step 3 Pile the pork mixture into small dishes.

1. Cut the pork into chunks, place in a food processor and process briefly.

2. Add the garlic, green onions (scallions), chilies, cashews, shrimp paste, soy, coriander (cilantro), pepper, and sugar to the processor and process again until all the ingredients are chopped and well combined.

3. Transfer the pork mixture to a bowl and beat in the coconut milk. Whisk the egg whites until standing in soft peaks, then fold into the mixture. Pile the pork mixture into four or six small dishes. Place in a steamer and steam for 20 minutes, or until the mixture is set and cooked through, then remove from the steamer and allow to cool.

4. To make the salad, combine the peppers and bean sprouts, and sprinkle with the lime juice and fish sauce.

5. Turn the pork out of the dishes and cut it into wedges. Serve with the pepper-and-bean-sprout salad and a hot dipping sauce of your choice (see Pastes and Dipping Sauces.)

Cook's Notes

Time
Preparation takes 20 minutes and cooking takes about 20 minutes.

Cook's Tip
Place a sheet of baking parchment or foil over the pork as it cooks, to prevent condensation dripping into the dishes.

CHICKEN AND PEANUT CURRY

This dish is sometimes known as dry chicken curry because of its thick sauce.

SERVES 4

1 pound chicken breasts, skinned and boned
Juice of 1 lemon
Juice of 1 lime
3 green chilies, seeded and chopped
4 tbsps oil
1 onion, chopped
¼ tsp ground cumin
¼ tsp ground coriander (cilantro)
4 tbsps ground roasted peanuts
⅔ cup chicken broth
⅔ cup thick coconut milk
6 tbsps freshly-grated coconut
1 tbsp sugar
1 tbsp fish sauce

1. Cut the chicken into bite-sized pieces and place in a shallow dish. Combine the lemon juice, lime juice, and chopped chilies and pour this over the chicken; toss until the chicken is coated and leave to marinate 1 hour.

2. Heat the oil in a wok and sauté the onion until softened and beginning to brown. Stir in the cumin and coriander (cilantro). Remove the chicken from the marinade with a slotted spoon and stir-fry quickly until browned.

3. Add the marinade and cook over a high heat for 2-3 minutes.

4. Stir in the ground roasted peanuts, then gradually add the broth and coconut milk. Add the grated coconut, sugar, and fish sauce, then simmer gently for 5 minutes or until the chicken is cooked through.

Step 2 Remove the chicken from the marinade and add to the ingredients in the wok. Quickly stir-fry the chicken until browned.

Step 3 Add the marinade from the chicken and cook over a high heat for 2-3 minutes.

Step 4 Stir the ground roasted peanuts into the wok.

Cook's Notes

Time
Preparation takes 10 minutes, plus 1 hour marinating. Cooking takes 15 minutes.

Variation
Use crunchy peanut butter instead of ground roasted peanuts.

SPICY GROUND BEEF
(LAAB ISAN)

This hot and spicy dish is a favorite in northern Thailand. If wished, you can remove the seeds from the chilies and reduce their quantity for a milder flavor.

SERVES 4

1 tbsp glutinous rice
1 tbsp oil
1 stem lemongrass, sliced
4 small red chilies, sliced
2 cloves garlic, chopped
1 tbsp grated fresh root ginger
1 pound lean ground beef
Juice of 1 lemon
2 tbsps fish sauce
1 tbsp chopped coriander (cilantro) leaves
Lime wedges, to garnish

Step 2 Pound the toasted rice in pestle and mortar, until it is almost ground to a powder.

Step 4 Add the beef to the wok and cook until it turns color, breaking it up as it cooks.

Step 1 Dry-fry the rice in a wok for 5-10 minutes or until golden on all sides.

1. Place the rice in a wok and dry-fry for 5-10 minutes until the grains are golden on all sides, shaking the wok as it cooks.

2. Pour the toasted rice into a pestle and mortar and pound until ground almost to a powder.

3. Heat the oil in the wok and stir-fry the lemongrass, chilies, garlic, and ginger for 3 minutes.

4. Add the beef and cook until the meat turns color, breaking it up as it cooks.

5. When the meat is cooked, sprinkle with lemon juice and fish sauce. Stir in the ground rice and cook it for 1 minute.

6. Transfer to a serving dish, scatter with the chopped coriander (cilantro) leaves, and garnish with lime wedges.

Cook's Notes

Time
Preparation takes 15 minutes and cooking takes 15-20 minutes.

Preparation
If you don't have a pestle and mortar, put the toasted rice in a plastic bag and crush with a rolling pin.

YELLOW CHICKEN CURRY
(KAENG KARRI KAI)

This easy-to-prepare curry is an example of the Indian
influence on traditional Thai cuisine.

SERVES 4

1 pound chicken breast, skinned and boned
2 tbsps oil
2 cloves garlic, sliced
1 onion, peeled and cut into wedges
3 tbsps Yellow Curry Paste, (see Pastes and
  Dipping Sauces)
2¼ cups thick coconut milk
1 small potato, peeled, and cut into chunks
2 kaffir lime leaves, shredded

1. Cut the chicken into even-sized chunks.

2. Heat the oil in a wok, and fry the garlic and onion for
3 minutes. Add the curry paste and fry 1 minute.

3. Stir in half the coconut milk and bring to the boil. Boil
rapidly for 5 minutes, stirring occasionally. Stir in the
remaining coconut milk, bring to the boil and add the

Step 3 Stir in half the
coconut milk and boil
for 5 minutes, stirring
occasionally.

Step 3 Stir in the
remaining coconut
milk and bring to the
boil.

Step 2 Fry the garlic
and onion for 3
minutes. Add the
curry paste and fry
for 1 minute.

potatoes and chicken.

4. Reduce the heat and simmer gently for 20-30
minutes, or until the chicken is cooked and the potato is
tender.

5. Spoon into serving dishes and sprinkle with the lime
leaves.

Cook's Notes

🕐 **Time**
Preparation takes 10 minutes
and cooking takes 30-40 minutes.

❀ **Serving Idea**
Accompany with Thai Steamed
Rice or Stir-Fried Thai Noodles.

BARBECUED PORK

Traditionally this dish is cooked on a charcoal burner
by the roadside, but it works just as well in the oven.

SERVES 4

4 cloves garlic, crushed
⅔ cup light soy sauce
2 tbsps dark brown sugar
1 tbsp grated fresh root ginger
1 tbsp chopped fresh coriander (cilantro)
4 whole star anise or 1 tsp ground anise
Red food coloring (optional)
2 pork fillets
2 tbsps oil
2 shallots, chopped
½ cup ground roasted peanuts
⅔ cup pork or chicken broth
1 tsp cornstarch mixed with 1 tsp water
Lime leaves and star anise, to garnish

Step 1 Mix together the garlic, soy, sugar, ginger, coriander, anise and food coloring.

Step 2 Add the pork to the marinade, turn it so that it is completely coated, and leave to marinate for at least 1 hour.

Step 3 Test the pork with a skewer, if it is cooked the juices will run clear.

1. Combine the garlic, soy, sugar, ginger, coriander, anise, and a few drops of food coloring, if used, to make a marinade.

2. Place the pork fillets in a shallow dish and add the marinade. Turn the pork over so that it is fully coated and leave to marinate for at least 1 hour, turning once.

3. Remove the meat from the marinade and place on a trivet in a roasting pan. Roast in an oven preheated to 375°F, for 20 minutes or until pork is cooked. Baste once or twice with some of the marinade during cooking. Test the pork with a skewer – the juices should run clear.

4. Just before the end of the roasting time, heat the oil in a wok and sauté the shallots until tender and beginning to brown. Stir in the ground peanuts, the remaining marinade, and the broth. Cook until simmering, then stir in the cornstarch mixture and cook a little longer until thickened.

5. To serve, slice the pork and pour the sauce over it. Garnish with lime leaves and star anise.

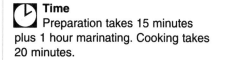

Cook's Notes

Time
Preparation takes 15 minutes plus 1 hour marinating. Cooking takes 20 minutes.

Preparation
The pork can be broiled or barbecued, if liked.

CHICKEN WITH CHILI AND BASIL

Three kinds of basil are used in Thailand. Bai Horapa is the closest to European basil. Look out for the other Thai varieties in Asian shops.

SERVES 4

4 chicken quarters, skinned
3 large red chilies, seeded and chopped
1 tbsp fresh coriander (cilantro) root and stem chopped
2 cloves garlic, crushed
3 tbsps oil
2 green chilies, sliced
2 tbsps fish sauce
1 tbsp oyster sauce (optional)
Small bunch basil, torn into small pieces
Chili "flowers," to garnish

Step 1 Cut the chicken quarters into smaller pieces using a large sharp knife or a cleaver.

1. Cut the chicken into smaller pieces using a large, sharp knife or a meat cleaver.

2. Pound the red chilies, coriander (cilantro), and garlic together in a pestle and mortar.

3. Heat the oil in a wok and fry the chicken until golden and almost cooked through. Remove from the pan.

4. Add the pounded chili mixture and fry for a few minutes. Return the chicken to the pan and add the green chilies, fish sauce, and oyster sauce if using. Cook over a medium heat for 5-10 minutes or until the chicken is completely cooked.

5. Stir in the basil leaves and serve garnished with chili "flowers."

Step 3 Fry the chicken pieces until golden and almost cooked through.

Step 4 Add the green chilies to the chicken in the wok.

Cook's Notes

Time
Preparation takes 20 minutes and cooking takes 20 minutes.

Cook's Tip
Tearing basil leaves rather than cutting them with a knife allows more flavor to be released.

MUSSAMAN CURRY

This curry illustrates the Indian influence on some of Thailand's cuisine.

SERVES 4

4 cardamom pods
½ tsp coriander (cilantro) seeds
½ tsp caraway seeds
2 whole cloves
5 small red chilies, chopped
1 clove garlic, crushed
1 stem lemongrass, roughly chopped
2 green onions (scallions), chopped
¼ tsp grated root ginger
¼ tsp ground nutmeg
1 tbsp oil
Oil for shallow frying
3 cups potatoes, peeled and cut into chunks
2-3 onions, peeled and cut into wedges
1½ pounds sirloin steak, cut into bite-sized chunks
1¾ cups thin coconut milk
2 tbsps dark brown sugar
1 tsp tamarind juice
Chopped coriander (cilantro), to garnish

1. Crush the cardamom pods with the side of a knife and remove the seeds.

2. Place the coriander (cilantro) seeds, caraway seeds, cardamom, and cloves in a wok and dry-fry for 1 minute, tossing frequently to prevent burning. Remove from the heat.

3. Mix the fried seeds, chilies, garlic, lemongrass, green onions (scallions), ginger, nutmeg, and oil together, and pound in a pestle and mortar.

4. Heat the oil for shallow frying in a wok and fry the potato and onion wedges for 5 minutes or until they

Step 1 Crush the cardamom pods with the side of a knife and remove the seeds.

Step 2 Dry-fry the spices in a wok for 1 minute.

begin to soften, then remove and set aside.

5. Add the meat to the pan and fry until browned. Stir in ½ cup of the coconut milk and simmer gently for 30 minutes or until meat is very tender.

6. Remove the meat from the wok with a slotted spoon and set aside. Add the chili mixture to the wok and boil rapidly for 5 minutes, then blend in the remaining milk.

7. Return the meat, onions and potatoes to the wok. Stir in the sugar and tamarind juice and cook gently for 20 minutes. Garnish with chopped coriander (cilantro).

Cook's Notes

Time
Preparation takes 25 minutes and cooking takes 1 hour.

Cook's Tip
Cut the steak across the grain to keep it tender.

Chapter 4

Pastes & Dipping Sauces

GREEN AND RED CURRY PASTES

Red and green curry pastes form the basis of most Thai curries.
Red curry paste is milder than the green.

MAKES ¼ CUP OF EACH

Green Curry Paste
16 green Serrano or other small chilies, chopped
3 cloves garlic, crushed
2 stems lemongrass, roughly chopped
3 green onions (scallions), chopped
1 tsp grated fresh root ginger
1 tsp coriander (cilantro) seeds
1 tsp caraway seeds
4 whole cloves
1 tsp ground nutmeg
1 tsp shrimp paste
3 tbsps oil

Red Curry Paste
12 small red chilies, chopped
3 cloves garlic, crushed
1 stem lemongrass, chopped
1 small onion, finely chopped
1 tsp grated fresh root ginger
2 tsps chopped coriander (cilantro) stems and root
Large pinch of cumin
1 tsp shrimp paste
2 tbsps oil

1. To make either the red or green curry paste, place the chilies, garlic, lemongrass, and onion in a pestle and mortar, and pound until the herbs are crushed and the juices blend.

2. Add all the remaining ingredients except the oil and continue to pound until a paste is formed. Finally blend in the oil.

3. Curry pastes can also be made in a spice-grinder or coffee grinder. Place all the ingredients in the grinder and blend to a paste.

Step 2 Blend the oil into the ingredients in the pestle and mortar.

Cook's Notes

Time
Preparation takes 15 minutes for each paste.

Cook's Tip
The pastes will keep for up to 1 month in the refrigerator.

Preparation
Store the paste in an airtight jar and refrigerate until required.

YELLOW CURRY PASTE

The turmeric in this curry paste gives curries a lovely golden hue.
This curry paste is not as hot as the red or green pastes.

MAKES ⅓ CUP

2 tbsps cumin seeds
2 tbsps coriander (cilantro) seeds
3 stems lemongrass, chopped
1 tbsp grated fresh root ginger
6 red chilies, seeded and chopped
1 tsp salt
3 cloves garlic, crushed
1 small shallot, finely chopped
1 tsp ground turmeric
1 tsp shrimp paste

1. Place the cumin and coriander (cilantro) seeds in a dry wok and dry-fry for 3-4 minutes, shaking the wok frequently to prevent the spices from burning. Remove from the heat and set aside.

2. Place the lemongrass and ginger in a large pestle and mortar and pound together until well crushed. Add the chilies and salt and continue pounding together for about 4 minutes.

3. Add the garlic and shallot and pound until broken down, then add the fried spices and turmeric. Finally, add the shrimp paste and continue to pound together until a smooth moist paste is produced.

NAM PRIK

This is a hot dipping sauce, also used in Vietnam, which can be served with most Thai dishes, especially those with a relatively mild flavor.

SERVES 4

1 tsp shrimp paste
1 tsp salt
1 tsp light brown sugar
4 cloves garlic, crushed
5 small red chilies, chopped
8 anchovy fillets, chopped
½ tbsp light soy sauce
Juice of ½ lime

1. Pound together the shrimp paste, salt, sugar, garlic, chilies, and anchovies to a smooth paste in a pestle and mortar or in a spice- or coffee-grinder.

2. Stir in the soy sauce and lime juice and transfer to a small bowl.

Cook's Notes

Time
Yellow Curry Paste: preparation takes 15 minutes.
Nam Prik: Preparation takes 10 minutes.

Cook's Tip
Yellow Curry Paste: store the paste in an airtight jar in the refrigerator until required. It will keep for up to 1 month.

Serving Idea
Nam Prik: serve with Pork Wrapped in Noodles or Mixed Vegetable Stir-Fry.

SWEET CHILI SAUCE

A delicious tangy sweet-and-sour chili sauce.

SERVES 4

½ cup canned plums, drained and pitted
1 tbsp oil
3 red chilies, chopped
1 clove garlic, crushed
1 tsp palm sugar
2 tbsps white wine vinegar
Fish sauce, to taste

1. Mince the plums very finely. This can be done in a food processor if wished.

2. Heat the oil in a small pan or wok and fry the chilies and garlic for 3 minutes, until just softened. Stir in the plums and the rest of the ingredients and heat through.

SWEET-AND-SOUR DIPPING SAUCE

Another popular dipping sauce that
can be served with a lot of Thai dishes.

SERVES 4

½ cup diced cucumber
¼ cup diced carrots
⅔ cup white wine vinegar
2 tbsps palm sugar
1 tsp chopped fresh coriander (cilantro)

1. Combine the cucumber and carrots.

2. Combine with all the other ingredients in a bowl and stir until the sugar dissolves.

Cook's Notes

Time
Preparation takes 10 minutes for each sauce.

Serving Idea
Sweet Chili Sauce: serve with Thai Spring Rolls or pork dishes.

Cook's Tip
Sweet-and-sour Dipping Sauce: this sauce is best served freshly made.

FISH SAUCE WITH CHILI

This is a good dipping sauce and can also be used in curries
and stir-fries to add spiciness and saltiness to the dish.

SERVES 4

4 tbsps fish sauce
1 tbsp lime juice
½ tsp palm sugar
6 small green chilies, sliced into circles
½ small shallot, finely chopped

1. Combine the fish sauce and lime juice in a small bowl. Add the sugar and stir until dissolved.

2. Add the prepared chilies and shallot and stir until well combined; leave to stand for at least 30 minutes before using.

NUOC CHAM

This sauce is delicious served with rice or Spicy Shrimp Wraps.

SERVES 4

1 tbsp lime juice
4 tbsps fish sauce
3 tbsps water
1 tsp palm sugar
1 red chili, seeded and shredded
1 tbsp grated carrot
1 tbsp chopped roasted peanuts

1. Combine the lime juice, fish sauce, and water in a small bowl, and add the sugar. Stir until the sugar dissolves.

2. Add the chili and grated carrot, then stir in the roasted peanuts.

Cook's Notes

Time
Fish Sauce with Chili: preparation takes 5 minutes, plus 30 minutes standing time.
Nuoc Cham: preparation takes 10 minutes.

Serving Idea
Fish Sauce with Chili: serve as a dipping sauce or pour it over rice.

Cook's Tip
Nuoc Cham: this sauce is best served freshly-made.

Chapter 5
Rice, Noodles, & Vegetables

THAI STEAMED RICE

Jasmine rice is a fragrant rice with a delicate flavor. Do not add salt during cooking as this will destroy the slightly nutty flavor.

SERVES 4-6

1 cup jasmine rice
2½ cups water

1. Rinse the rice under running water and drain it.

2. Place the rice and the measured water in a saucepan and bring gently to the boil.

Step 3 Cook the rice gently with the measured water for 10 minutes or until the water has been absorbed.

3. Stir the rice, cover, reduce the heat, and simmer gently for 10 minutes or until the water has been absorbed.

4. Line a steamer with a piece of cheesecloth and pile the rice into the steamer. Steam over gently simmering water for 30 minutes.

5. Stand the rice for a few minutes, then fluff up gently with a fork.

Step 4 Line a steamer with a piece of cheesecloth.

Step 4 Pile the rice into the steamer and cook over gently simmering water for 30 minutes.

Cook's Notes

🕐 **Time**
Preparation takes 5 minutes and cooking takes about 40 minutes.

Serving Idea
Serve as an accompaniment to a Thai curry.

BAKED PINEAPPLE RICE
(KHAO OP SAPPAROD)

This attractively presented rice dish is from Bangkok and the Central Plains.

SERVES 6

1 pineapple
2 tbsps oil
1 clove garlic, crushed
4 shallots, chopped
1 tbsp Yellow Curry Paste (see Pastes and
   Dipping Sauces)
1 pound cooked rice
⅔ cup thick coconut milk
2 tbsps raisins
2 tbsps toasted cashew nuts
Chili "flowers," to garnish

Step 4 Pile the rice mixture into the pineapple shells.

Step 4 Wrap the pineapple leaves in foil to prevent them from burning.

Step 1 Cut the pineapple in half and scoop out the flesh to leave two shells with a thin border of flesh attached.

1. Cut the pineapple in half lengthwise, keeping the leaves attached. Scoop out the flesh using a tablespoon and a paring knife, to leave two shells with a thin border of flesh attached. Chop half the flesh to use later in the dish (the rest of the pineapple is not needed for this recipe.)

2. Heat the oil in a wok and fry the garlic and shallots

until softened. Stir in the curry paste and fry for 1 minute.

3. Add the rice and toss together with the shallot mixture. Stir in the coconut milk, raisins, chopped pineapple, and cashew nuts.

4. Pile the rice mixture into the pineapple shells. Wrap the pineapple leaves in foil to prevent them from burning and place on a cookie sheet.

5. Bake in a oven preheated to 325°F, for 20 minutes. Remove from the foil and serve garnished with chili "flowers."

Cook's Notes

Time
Preparation takes 20 minutes and cooking takes about 25 minutes.

Cook's Tip
If the pineapple shells won't stand firmly upright, cut a thin slice from the bottom.

THAI FRIED RICE (KHAO PAD)

You can experiment with adding different fresh vegetables to the rice according to what you have to hand.

SERVES 4-6

About 1 tbsp oil
1 egg, beaten
1 tbsp thin coconut milk
1 cup chicken breast, skinned and cut into small
  pieces
⅔ cup raw, peeled shrimp
1 small red or green chili, seeded and chopped
1 tbsp Red or Green Curry Paste (see Pastes and
  Dipping Sauces)
2 tbsps fish sauce
3 cups cooked rice
1 cup long beans, cut into 1-inch lengths
6 green onions (scallions), sliced diagonally
Chili "flowers," to garnish

1. Heat a wok and brush with a little oil. Beat the egg and coconut milk and pour into the wok. Swirl the wok so that the egg coats it, to form a thin omelet.

2. Cook for a minute until just brown on the underside then flip over and cook the other side.

3. Remove from the wok and allow to cool slightly. Roll up and cut into thin strips; set aside.

4. Heat a little more oil in the wok and add the chicken and shrimp. Cook quickly, stirring frequently.

5. Add the chili, curry paste, and fish sauce to the pan and heat until sizzling hot. Stir in the rice, beans, and green onions (scallions).

6. Reduce the heat slightly and cook, stirring constantly, until the rice is hot.

Step 1 Pour the egg-and-coconut mixture into the hot wok and swirl so that it coats the wok and forms a thin omelet.

Step 3 Shred the rolled omelet into thin strips.

Step 7 Garnish the rice with the shredded omelet and chili "flowers."

7. Pile into a serving dish and garnish with the shredded omelet and chili "flowers."

Cook's Notes

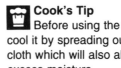

Time
Preparation takes 15 minutes and cooking takes 15 minutes.

Cook's Tip
Before using the cooked rice, cool it by spreading out on a clean cloth which will also absorb all the excess moisture.

THAI RICE SALAD (KHAO YAM)

A delicious and attractive salad from southern Thailand.

SERVES 4

1½ cups cooked rice
½ cucumber
1 grapefruit
6 green onions (scallions)
1-inch piece fresh root ginger
2 tbsps unsweetened shredded coconut
½ cup bean sprouts
2 tbsps dried shrimp, chopped
2 stems lemongrass, thinly sliced

Sauce
½ cup fish sauce
4 tbsps lime juice
2 tbsps light brown sugar

1. Divide the rice into four and press a quarter of the rice into an individual soufflé dish or teacup. Unmold onto an individual serving plate. Repeat with the remaining rice.

2. Cut the cucumber into quarters and slice thinly. Peel

Step 4 To serve, each diner scatters the salad ingredients over their portion of rice.

the grapefruit, discarding the white part, and segment the flesh. Slice the green onions (scallions) diagonally. Peel the ginger and cut into thin sticks.

3. Arrange the various salad ingredients separately on a serving platter. Combine the ingredients for the sauce and pour into one large or four small dishes.

4. Each diner sprinkles some of the individual ingredients over their mound of rice. They then pour a little sauce over the top.

Step 1 Unmold the rice onto individual serving plates.

Step 4 The sauce is drizzled over just before serving.

Cook's Notes

🕐 **Time**
Preparation takes 20 minutes.

Variation
Alternatively, all the salad ingredients can be mixed together and tossed in the sauce just before serving.

FRIED RICE WITH CRAB
(KHAO PAD POO)

For fried rice dishes such as this use cooked rice
which has been chilled, as it will break up more readily.

SERVES 4

2 tbsps oil
2 eggs, beaten
2 shallots, chopped
2 cloves garlic, crushed
3 cups cooked rice
2 small red chilies, sliced
1 cup canned crabmeat, drained
2 tbsps fish sauce
Lime wedges, to garnish

Step 2 Slice the rolled up omelets into thin shreds.

Step 3 Add the cooked rice to the wok and stir-fry for 2 minutes.

Step 1 Add half the egg to the wok and swirl thinly to coat and form a thin omelet.

1. Heat 1 tbsp of the oil in a wok and add about half the egg. Swirl to thinly coat the wok and form a thin omelet. Cook until the egg sets, then remove from the wok. Repeat with the remaining egg.

2. Roll up each omelet, shred thinly, and set aside.

3. Heat the remaining oil in the wok and fry the shallots and garlic until softened. Add the rice and fry, stirring frequently, for 2 minutes.

4. Stir in the chilies, crabmeat, and fish sauce and stir-fry for 2-3 minutes or until the rice and crab are hot.

5. Toss with the egg strips and serve garnished with lime wedges.

Cook's Notes

Time
Preparation takes 10 minutes and cooking takes 10 minutes.

Serving Idea
Serve accompanied by a dipping sauce such as Fish Sauce with Chili.

SHRIMP PASTE FRIED RICE
(KHAO CLOOK GAPI)

This is a strongly flavored rice dish which is
best served with steamed vegetables.

SERVES 4

2 tbsps oil
1 tbsp dried shrimp
4 cloves garlic, crushed
2 red chilies, seeded and chopped
3 cups cooked rice
2 tbsps shrimp paste
2 eggs, beaten
4 green onions (scallions), sliced
3 tbsps fish sauce
Coriander (cilantro) leaves, to garnish

1. Heat the oil in a wok and fry the dried shrimp for
about 30 seconds; remove and set aside to drain on
kitchen paper.

2. Add the garlic and chilies and fry until softened.

3. Stir in the rice and shrimp paste and stir-fry for 5
minutes or until heated through.

4. Add the beaten eggs and green onions (scallions)
and cook over a low heat, stirring until the egg is
cooked. Add the fish sauce.

5. To serve, sprinkle with the fried dried shrimp and
garnish with coriander (cilantro) leaves.

Step 4 Add the
beaten egg and
green onions
(scallions) to the
rice. Cook over a low
heat, stirring until the
egg is cooked.

Step 1 Fry the dried
shrimp for about 30
seconds.

Step 5 Sprinkle with
the fried dried shrimp
to serve.

Cook's Notes

Time
Preparation takes 10 minutes
and cooking takes 15 minutes.

Serving Idea
Serve with vegetables such as
steamed bok choy or long beans.

SPICY RICE WITH CHICKEN

This spicy side dish can also be served as a light lunch or supper dish.

SERVES 4

8 ounces cooked chicken
1 cup long beans, cut into 1-inch lengths
1 tbsp oil
2 tbsps Red Curry Paste (see Pastes and
    Dipping Sauces)
2 cups cooked rice
2 tbsps fish sauce
1 tsp palm sugar
Chili "flowers" and green onions (scallions), to garnish

1. Shred the chicken finely. Blanch the beans in boiling water for 5 minutes or until just tender.

2. Heat the oil in a wok and fry the curry paste for 3-4 minutes, stirring frequently.

3. Add the chicken and rice to the wok and stir-fry for 5 minutes, tossing frequently.

Step 2 Fry the curry paste for 3-4 minutes stirring frequently.

4. Add the beans and cook a further 2 minutes or until all the ingredients are heated through.

5. Mix together the fish sauce and sugar; stir until the sugar dissolves. Add to the wok. Toss well and serve garnished with chili "flowers" and green onions (scallions).

Step 1 Cut the cooked chicken into thin shreds using a sharp knife.

Step 4 Add the blanched beans to the ingredients in the wok and cook for 2 minutes, or until all the ingredients are hot.

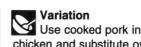

Cook's Notes

Time
Preparation takes 10 minutes and cooking takes 15 minutes.

Variation
Use cooked pork instead of chicken and substitute oyster sauce for the fish sauce.

STIR-FRIED THAI NOODLES
(PAD THAI)

This is a popular basic Thai dish that has as many variations as there are Thai cooks.
SERVES 4

6 ounces rice noodles
4 tbsps oil
1 cup cubed tofu
3 cloves garlic, crushed
2 tbsps dried shrimp
3 tbsps chopped pickled turnip
4 tbsps fish sauce
1 tbsp palm sugar
1 tbsp soy sauce
2 tbsps tamarind juice
2 eggs, beaten
1 tbsp chopped garlic chives
2 tbsps roasted peanuts, chopped
2 cups bean sprouts
Chili strips, to garnish

1. Soak the rice noodles in boiling water for 10-15 minutes or until softened, then drain and set aside.

2. Heat the oil in a wok and fry the tofu cubes until browned on all sides. Remove with a slotted spoon and set aside.

3. Add the garlic and dried shrimp to the wok and stir-fry for 2 minutes. Reduce the heat and add the noodles. Cook for 5 minutes, tossing the ingredients frequently. Add the pickled turnip, fish sauce, sugar, soy sauce, and tamarind juice and cook for 2 minutes.

4. Add the beaten egg and cook, tossing the ingredients together until the egg sets. Stir in the tofu, garlic chives, peanuts, and beans sprouts. Garnish with chili strips and serve immediately.

Step 1 Soak the rice noodles in boiling water for 10-15 minutes or until softened.

Step 2 Fry the tofu cubes in a wok until browned on all sides.

Step 3 Add the noodles to the ingredients in the wok and cook for 5 minutes, tossing frequently.

Cook's Notes

Time
Preparation takes 10 minutes, plus 10-15 minutes soaking. Cooking takes about 15 minutes.

Variation
Cashew nuts may be used instead of peanuts and sliced bamboo shoots instead of bean sprouts.

STIR-FRIED GLASS NOODLES WITH CHICKEN

Serve as part of a Thai meal or as a light supper snack for 2-3 people.
SERVES 4

1 chicken breast, skinned and boned
2 tbsps oyster sauce
2 tbsps fish sauce
1 tbsp soy sauce
1 tsp palm sugar
½ large red chili, seeded and chopped
½ tsp grated fresh root ginger
6 ounces cellophane noodles
2 tbsps oil
2 cloves garlic, crushed
1 red onion, sliced
Coriander (cilantro) leaves, to garnish

Step 3 Add the chicken and the marinade to the garlic and onion in a wok and stir-fry for about 10 minutes or until the chicken is cooked through.

Step 4 Add the drained noodles to the wok and toss over a low heat until heated through.

Step 1 Marinate the chicken slices in the oyster sauce, fish sauce, soy, sugar, chili, and ginger.

1. Cut the chicken into thin slices. Combine the oyster sauce, fish sauce, soy, sugar, chili, and ginger in a shallow dish. Add the chicken and toss until well coated. Leave to marinate for 20 minutes.

2. Soak the noodles in boiling water for 5 minutes, until softened. Drain and set aside.

3. Heat the oil in a wok and fry the garlic and onion until just softened. Add the chicken and the marinade and stir-fry for about 10 minutes or until the chicken is cooked through.

4. Add the noodles to the wok and toss over a low heat until heated through. Pile onto a serving dish and garnish with coriander leaves.

Cook's Notes

Time
Preparation takes 5 minutes plus 20 minutes marinating. Cooking takes about 15 minutes.

Cook's Tip
Partially freeze the chicken to make slicing easier. Cut the chicken across the grain to keep the meat tender.

SPICY STEAMED PORK WITH NOODLES

In Thailand, noodle dishes like this are served as part of the main course or as a snack at any time of the day.

SERVES 4

1 cup ground pork
1 tsp ground coriander (cilantro)
1 tsp ground cumin
1 tsp ground turmeric
1 bunch bok choy, washed
1-2 tbsps Red or Green Curry Paste (see Pastes and
    Dipping Sauces)
1 tsp shrimp paste
⅔ cup thick coconut milk
6 ounces egg noodles
Chopped fresh coriander (cilantro), to garnish

1. Place the ground pork and spices in a food processor and process until very finely chopped. Shape the pork mixture into small balls using dampened hands.

2. Tear the bok choy into large pieces and place in a heat-proof dish that will fit into a steamer. Arrange the meatballs on top.

3. Combine the curry paste, shrimp paste, and coconut milk and pour this over the meatballs. Cover and steam for 20 minutes.

4. Meanwhile, cook the noodles as directed on the package. Mix the noodles with the pork and bok choy or arrange noodles on a plate and pile the pork mixture on top. Garnish with a sprinkling of chopped coriander leaves.

Step 2 Tear the bok choy into large pieces and place in a heatproof dish that will fit into a steamer.

Step 3 Pour the curry paste, shrimp paste, and coconut milk mixture over the meatballs in the steamer. Cover and steam for 20 minutes.

Step 4 While the meatballs are cooking, cook the noodles as directed on the package.

Cook's Notes

 Time
Preparation takes 20 minutes and cooking takes 20 minutes.

 Preparation
The pork can be mixed with the spices by hand. Add a little beaten egg if necessary, to help bind the mixture together.

138

TOFU WITH CRISPY NOODLES

Tofu is an ideal substitute for meat or fish and
therefore perfect for vegetarian main courses.

SERVES 4

Oil for deep-frying
4 ounces rice noodles
1 cup tofu, drained and patted dry
2 carrots, peeled and sliced
1 cup broccoli flowerets
2 sticks celery, sliced
1 onion, peeled and cut into wedges
1 tsp shrimp paste
2 tbsps light soy sauce
3 tbsps white wine vinegar
2 tbsps dark brown sugar
1 tsp grated fresh root ginger

1. Heat the oil to 360°F in a wok. Add the rice noodles in small batches, and fry for a few seconds, turning them. The rice will puff up immediately.

2. Remove from the oil and drain well on kitchen paper.

3. Cut the tofu into cubes and fry for a few minutes until browned on all sides. Remove from the oil and set aside.

4. Pour off most of the oil, add the carrots, broccoli, celery, and onion to the wok and stir-fry for 2 minutes, or until the vegetables are cooked but still crisp.

5. Stir in the shrimp paste, soy sauce, vinegar, sugar, and ginger. Return the vermicelli and tofu to the wok, toss to mix and serve immediately.

Step 2 As soon as the rice has puffed up remove it from the oil and drain on kitchen paper.

Step 1 Add the rice noodles in small batches to the hot oil in the wok.

Step 3 Fry the cubed tofu for a few minutes until browned on all sides, then remove from the oil and drain well.

Cook's Notes

Time
Preparation takes 10 minutes and cooking takes 10 minutes.

Variation
Use smoked tofu for a different flavor.

CHAING MAI NOODLES (KHAO SOI)

Originally from Burma, this dish has evolved into one with a distinctive Thai flavor.

SERVES 4-6

2 tbsps oil
2 cloves garlic, crushed
4 shallots, chopped
1 tbsp Red Curry Paste (see Pastes and
    Dipping Sauces)
½ tsp ground turmeric
Pinch of ground cumin
Pinch of ground coriander (cilantro)
1 cup coconut milk
8 ounces fillet or sirloin steak, thinly sliced
5 tbsps fish sauce
2 tbsps palm sugar
1 tbsp soy sauce
2 tbsps lime juice
1 tbsp garlic chives, chopped
1 pound fresh egg noodles
Chili "flowers" and crispy egg noodles (optional),
    to garnish

1. Heat the oil in a wok and fry the garlic and shallots until softened.

2. Stir in the curry paste, turmeric, cumin, and coriander (cilantro). Stir-fry for 1 minute.

3. Add the coconut milk and bring to the boil, reduce the heat and add the beef. Simmer for 15-20 minutes or

Step 3 Add the beef to the ingredients in the wok and simmer for 10-15 minutes or until the beef is tender.

until the beef is cooked.

4. Stir in the fish sauce, sugar, soy, lime juice, and garlic chives.

5. Meanwhile, cook the egg noodles in boiling water for 1 minute. Drain and arrange on a serving dish. Spoon the beef on top and serve garnished with chili "flowers" and crispy noodles if wished.

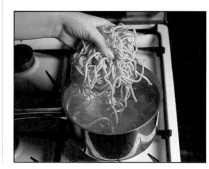

Step 5 While the beef is cooking, cook the fresh egg noodles in boiling water for 1 minute.

Cook's Notes

Time
Preparation takes 20 minutes and cooking takes about 20 minutes.

Cook's Tip
Cut the steak across the grain to keep it tender.

Preparation
To make the noodle garnish, deep-fry a few of the cooked egg noodles until crispy.

STIR-FRIED BABY CORN WITH MUSHROOMS

Serve this tasty vegetable dish as part of a complete Thai meal.

SERVES 4

2 tbsps oil
2 cloves garlic, crushed
4 shallots, chopped
1 pound baby sweetcorn, cut in half lengthways
1 cup snow peas
1 cup canned straw mushroom
1 tbsp grated galangal
½ tsp dried chili flakes
1 tbsp fish sauce
1 tbsp soy sauce

1. Heat the oil in a wok and fry the garlic and shallots until softened.

Step 1 Fry the garlic and shallots in the oil until softened.

Step 2 Stir in the baby corn cobs and cook for 5 minutes, then add the snow peas and cook for a further 2 minutes.

Step 3 Stir in the mushrooms, galangal, and chili. Stir-fry for 2 minutes.

2. Stir in the baby corn cobs and cook for 5 minutes, add the snow peas and continue cooking for 2 minutes.

3. Stir in the mushrooms, galangal and chili and stir-fry for 2 minutes. Sprinkle with the fish and soy sauce and serve.

Cook's Notes

Time
Preparation takes 10 minutes and cooking takes about 10 minutes.

Cook's Tip
This makes an original vegetarian entrée for 2 if the fish sauce is omitted.

LONG BEANS IN COCONUT MILK

In this recipe, the long beans are lightly cooked and should still be slightly crunchy when served.

SERVES 4-6

1 pound long beans
1 tbsp oil
2 stems lemongrass, sliced
1-inch piece galangal, sliced into thin sticks
1 large red chili, seeded and chopped
1¼ cups thin coconut milk
Chili "flowers," to garnish

Step 1 Cut the beans into 2-inch pieces.

1. Top and tail the beans and cut into 2-inch pieces.

2. Heat the oil in a wok and stir-fry the lemongrass, galangal, and chili for 1 minute.

3. Add the coconut milk and bring to the boil. Boil for 3 minutes.

4. Stir in the beans, reduce the heat, and simmer for 6 minutes. Garnish with chili "flowers" and serve immediately.

Step 2 Stir-fry the lemongrass, galangal, and chili for 1 minute.

Step 3 Add the coconut milk to the wok. Bring to the boil and boil for 3 minutes.

Cook's Notes

Time
Preparation takes 10 minutes and cooking takes 7 minutes.

Variation
Substitute snow peas for the beans and reduce the cooking time to 2-3 minutes.

SAUTÉED BEAN SPROUTS

A simple vegetable dish which can be served with a
hot dipping sauce if wished or as a foil to a hot curry.

SERVES 4

2 tbsps oil
8 green onions (scallions), thickly sliced
3 cups bean sprouts, rinsed and drained
⅔ cup cooked, peeled shrimp (optional)
½ small head of Chinese (Nappa) cabbage, shredded
1 tbsp fish sauce

1. Heat the oil in a wok until sizzling then add the green onions (scallions), bean sprouts, and shrimp, if using. Stir-fry for 1-2 minutes.

2. Add the Chinese (Nappa) cabbage and toss over a

Step 2 Add the Chinese (Nappa) cabbage and toss over a high heat for about 1 minute or until just beginning to wilt.

high heat for 1 minute or until just beginning to wilt.

3. Stir in the fish sauce and serve immediately with a dipping sauce of your choice.

Step 1 Stir-fry the green onions (scallions), bean sprouts, and shrimp in the sizzling oil for 1-2 minutes.

Step 3 Stir in the fish sauce and serve immediately.

Cook's Notes

Time
Preparation takes 5 minutes and cooking takes 5 minutes.

Cook's Tip
Use fresh bean sprouts rather than canned for this recipe.

CUCUMBER SALAD

Salads are an important part of a Thai meal. They are usually carefully arranged rather than simply tossed together.

SERVES 4

1 cucumber
6 romaine lettuce leaves
1 red bell pepper, sliced crosswise
1 tbsp roasted peanuts

Dressing
2 tbsps lime juice
1 tbsp fish sauce
1 tsp sugar
1 small red or green chili, seeded and chopped
2 tsps chopped coriander (cilantro) leaves

1. Cut the cucumber in half lengthwise and scoop out the seeds with a teaspoon.

2. Cut the cucumber into slices about ¼-inch-thick.

3. Arrange the lettuce leaves on a serving platter and scatter the pepper rings around the edge. Pile the cucumber into the center. Sprinkle with the roasted peanuts.

4. To make the dressing, whisk all the ingredients together with a fork or place in a small screw-top jar and shake well.

5. Just before serving sprinkle the dressing over the salad.

Step 1 Cut the cucumber in half lengthwise and scoop out the seeds with a teaspoon.

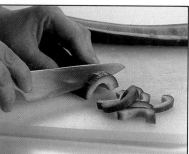

Step 2 Cut the cucumber crosswise into slices about ¼-inch-thick.

Step 4 To make the dressing, whisk all the ingredients together with a fork, or place in a small screw-top jar and shake well.

Cook's Notes

🕐 **Time**
Preparation takes 10 minutes.

🍳 **Cook's Tip**
Do not add the dressing to the salad until serving time.

GREEN PAPAYA SALAD

Originating in the northeast of Thailand this dish is now popular all over the country.

SERVES 4-6

1 tbsp dried shrimp
4 small green chilies, sliced
3 cloves garlic, crushed
1 shallot, chopped
1 firm, green papaya
1 tsp palm sugar
2 tbsps fish sauce
2 tbsps tamarind juice

Step 3 Cut the papaya in half, remove the seeds, and peel with a vegetable peeler.

Step 1 Grind the dried shrimp in a pestle and mortar until well crushed.

Step 3 Grate the papaya flesh into a mixing bowl.

1. Place the dried shrimp in a pestle and mortar and grind until well crushed; remove and set aside.

2. Place the chilies, garlic, and shallot in the pestle and mortar and pound until well bruised and the juices begin to blend.

3. Cut the papaya in half and remove the seeds. Peel it, using a vegetable peeler, and grate the papaya flesh

into a mixing bowl.

4. Combine the sugar, fish sauce, and tamarind juice and stir until the sugar dissolves.

5. Add this to the papaya along with the chili mixture and toss until well mixed. Chill until required.

6. Transfer to a serving platter. Sprinkle with the crushed shrimp just before serving.

Cook's Notes

Time
Preparation takes 20 minutes plus chilling.

Preparation
Use a coarse grater for preparing the papaya.

MIXED VEGETABLE STIR-FRY

Very fresh vegetables cooked quickly and simply play a
large part in Thai cuisine. This dish is an excellent example.

SERVES 4

Prik Dong
6 red or green chilies
6 tbsps white wine vinegar

2 tbsps oil
3 cloves garlic, crushed
1 shallot, sliced
½ cup each small cauliflower
  and broccoli flowerets
1 small red pepper, sliced
½ cup snow peas
½ cup baby baby corn cobs
½ cup long beans, cut into 2-inch lengths
2 carrots, peeled and sliced
⅓ cup straw mushrooms
2 tsps palm sugar
1 tbsp light soy sauce

1. Slice the chilies diagonally and combine with the vinegar in a small bowl. Use as a dipping sauce for the vegetables.

2. Heat the oil in a wok and add all the vegetables at once.

3. Stir-fry for 4 minutes until the vegetables are cooked but still crisp.

4. Stir the sugar into the soy sauce and add to the wok. Toss well and serve. Serve with the dipping sauce.

Step 1 Slice the chilies diagonally

Step 2 Heat the oil in a large wok and add all the vegetables at once. Stir-fry for 4 minutes.

Step 4 Add the sugar and soy to the wok. Toss well and serve.

Cook's Notes

Time
Preparation takes 15 minutes
and cooking takes 4-6 minutes.

Cook's Tip
Use the dipping sauce with
noodles as well as vegetables.

TOFU SALAD

This dish can also be served hot – return the tofu to the wok
and heat through, then serve immediately.

SERVES 4

6 tbsps oil
1 cup cubed tofu
2 cloves garlic, crushed
½ cup broccoli flowerets
½ cup snow peas
1 tbsp soy sauce
1 tsp salted black beans
½ tsp palm sugar
6 tbsps vegetable broth
½ tsp cornstarch

1. Heat the oil in a wok and fry the tofu until golden on all sides. Remove with a slotted spoon and cool, then refrigerate until required.

2. Pour off most of the oil. Add the garlic and fry until softened. Stir in the broccoli and snow peas, and stir-fry until just tender.

Step 3 Add the soy, black beans, and sugar and fry for 1 minute.

3. Add the soy, black beans, and sugar and fry for 1 minute.

4. Mix a little of the broth with the cornstarch and add the remaining broth-and-cornstarch mixture to the wok. Cook until the sauce thickens slightly.

5. Transfer to a serving dish and chill until required. To serve, scatter the tofu cubes over the cooked vegetables.

Step 2 Stir-fry the broccoli and snow peas until just tender.

Step 4 Blend a little of the broth with the cornstarch and add to the wok with the rest of the broth. Cook until the sauce thickens slightly.

Cook's Notes

Time
Preparation takes 15 minutes and cooking takes about 10 minutes.

Variation
Use smoked tofu for a different flavor. Cooked chicken or shrimp can be substituted for the tofu.

Chapter 6
Desserts

Thai Fruit Platter • Sticky Rice with Mango and Star Fruit

Thai Coconut Custards • Black Sticky Rice

Coconut and Banana Pancakes • Mango Ice Cream

Bananas in Coconut Milk • Tapioca with Golden Threads

THAI FRUIT PLATTER WITH COCONUT SAUCE

Usually, a Thai meal ends with fresh fruit. Here a selection of fruit is served with a simple coconut sauce.

SERVES 4

Selection of Thai fruit such as:
Lychee
Rambutan
Mango
Pineapple
Watermelon
Honeydew melon
Ripe papaya
Starfruit (carambola)
Banana
Lemon juice

Coconut Sauce
¾ cup thick coconut milk
2 tbsp superfine sugar

1. Prepare the fruit. Peel lychees or rambutans, starting at the stem end.

2. Cut mango in half either side of the stone, peel and slice into fingers.

3. Cut the pineapple into wedges, peeled if wished.

4. Cut watermelon, melon, and papaya in half and discard the seeds. Peel and slice.

5. Slice starfruit crosswise.

6. Cut bananas diagonally into chunks and toss them in lemon juice to stop them from browning.

7. Arrange the fruit on a serving platter.

8. Make the sauce by combining the coconut milk and sugar. Pour this over the fruit or serve separately in a bowl or jug.

Step 1 Peel the lychees, starting at the stem end.

Step 2 Cut the mango in half either side of the stone. Peel the fruit and slice the flesh into fingers.

Step 4 Cut the papaya in half and discard the seeds. Peel and slice the flesh.

Cook's Notes

 Time
Preparation takes 20-30 minutes.

Cook's Tip
Chill the fruit and coconut sauce well, before serving.

STICKY RICE WITH MANGO AND STARFRUIT

Sweet, sticky rice is used as the basis for many Thai desserts.
This delicious version is served with tropical fruits.

SERVES 4

1 cup raw sticky rice
1¾ cups thick coconut milk
3 tbsps sugar
Pinch of salt
1 mango
1 starfruit

Step 1 Soak the rice overnight in cold water.

1. Soak the rice overnight in cold water.

2. Line the top of a steamer with cheesecloth. Drain the rice and place it in the steamer. Cover and steam for 25 minutes. The rice should be just tender but not fully cooked.

3. Combine the coconut milk, sugar, and salt in a saucepan and heat gently. Stir in the steamed rice and simmer for 2 minutes.

Step 2 Line the top of a steamer with cheesecloth. Add the drained rice, cover, and steam for 25 minutes.

4. Remove from the heat, cover, and leave to stand for 15 minutes. The rice will continue to cook.

5. Cut the mango in half as close to the stone as possible. Remove the peel, and slice the flesh. Slice the star fruit crosswise.

6. Arrange the fruit and rice attractively on serving dishes.

Step 3 Add the steamed rice to the hot coconut milk, sugar, and salt in the saucepan. Cover and simmer for 2 minutes then remove from the heat and leave to stand for 15 minutes.

Cook's Notes

Time
Preparation takes 10 minutes, plus overnight soaking. Cooking takes 27 minutes, plus 15 minutes standing.

Cook's Tip
Make this dish using whatever tropical fruits are available.

THAI COCONUT CUSTARDS

This is one of the best known and most loved of Thai desserts.

SERVES 6

4 eggs
1¼ cups thick coconut milk
4 tbsps superfine sugar
½ tsp jasmine water
Shredded coconut and lime peel twists, to decorate

1. Place the eggs, coconut milk, sugar, and jasmine water in a bowl and whisk together until slightly frothy.

2. Pour into a shallow, heatproof dish, that will fit into the top of a steamer.

3. Steam over gently simmering water for 30-40 minutes or until the custard is just set. If the custard cooks too quickly, it will become rubbery in texture.

4. Remove from the steamer and allow to cool. Cut into wedges or blocks and decorate with the coconut, grated lime zest, and lime twists.

Step 2 Pour the mixture into a shallow heatproof dish that will fit into the top of a steamer.

Step 1 Place the eggs, coconut milk, sugar and jasmine water in a bowl and whisk together until slightly frothy.

Step 3 Steam the custard over gently simmering water for 30-40 minutes or until just set.

Cook's Notes

🕐 **Time**
Preparation takes 5 minutes and cooking takes 30-40 minutes.

📐 **Preparation**
The custard is cooked when the tip of a knife blade inserted into the center comes out clean.

BLACK STICKY RICE

Look out for this rice in Thai or Oriental food stores. You can use white sticky rice if it is unavailable.

SERVES 6

1½ cups black glutinous rice
5 cups water
⅔ cups sugar
1½ cups thick coconut milk
6 tbsps grated fresh coconut

1. Rinse the rice under plenty of running water and drain well.

2. Place the rice in a large saucepan with the measured water. Bring gently to the boil, stir, and reduce the heat. Simmer for 45 minutes or until rice is tender, stirring occasionally.

3. If any water is left in the rice, drain and discard it. If the rice is not tender but there is not enough water, add a little more water and continue to cook until the rice is

Step 4 Stir in 3 tbsps of the sugar and 1¼ cups of the coconut milk and simmer gently for 10 minutes.

done. Transfer to a clean saucepan.

4. Stir in 3 tbsps of the sugar and 1¼ cups of the coconut milk. Simmer gently for 10 minutes.

5. Combine the remaining sugar and coconut milk with the coconut flesh in a small pan and heat gently.

6. Spoon the rice into serving bowls and top with the coconut mixture. Serve at once.

Step 3 When the rice is cooked and tender, drain if necessary and transfer to a clean pan.

Step 5 Combine the remaining sugar, coconut milk, and coconut flesh in a small pan and heat gently.

Cook's Notes

Time
Preparation takes 15 minutes and cooking takes 55 minutes.

Variation
For chocolate sticky rice, add unsweetened cocoa to taste in Step 4.

COCONUT AND BANANA PANCAKES

These pancakes are delicious served warm or cold.

SERVES 4

½ cup rice flour
Pinch of salt
2 eggs
1½ cups thin coconut milk
Green food coloring (optional)
2 tbsps unsweetened shredded coconut

Filling
2 tbsps lime juice
Grated rind of ½ lime
1 tsp sugar
1 tbsp unsweetened shredded coconut
2 bananas

Oil for frying

Step 1 Place the flour and salt in a mixing bowl and make a well in the center. Drop the eggs and a little of the milk into the well.

Step 3 Gradually beat in the remaining coconut milk.

Step 5 Spoon about 4 tbsps of pancake batter into the pan and swirl to coat.

1. Place the flour and the salt in a mixing bowl and make a well in the center. Drop the eggs and a little of the coconut milk into the well.

2. Using a wooden spoon beat well, slowly incorporating the flour until you have a smooth, thick paste.

3. Gradually beat in the remaining coconut milk. Stir in a few drops of food coloring, if used. Allow to stand for 20 minutes.

4. Meanwhile, make the filling. Mix together the lime juice, rind, sugar, and coconut. Slice the bananas and toss them in the mixture.

5. Stir the coconut into the pancake batter. Heat a little oil in an 8-inch heavy-based skillet. Pour off the excess and spoon in about 4 tbsps of the batter. Swirl to coat the pan. Cook for about 1 minute or until the underside is golden.

6. Flip or toss the pancake over and cook other side. Slide the pancake out of the pan and keep warm. Repeat until all the batter is used. Fill the pancakes with the banana mixture and serve immediately.

Cook's Notes

Time
Preparation takes 15 minutes, plus 20 minutes standing time. Cooking takes 15 minutes.

Serving Idea
Fold the pancakes into quarters and spoon some filling inside or divide filling between the pancakes and roll up.

MANGO ICE CREAM

The cool, smooth, creaminess of this delicious ice cream
makes it the perfect end to a Thai meal.

SERVES 8

1¾ cups thick coconut milk
3 egg yolks
4 tbsps sugar
1 cup whipping cream
3 mangoes, peeled and pitted
Toasted flaked almonds, to decorate

1. Heat the coconut milk in a saucepan until very hot, but not boiling.

2. Beat together the egg yolks and sugar in a bowl, add a few tablespoons of the hot coconut milk and stir well.

3. Stir this into the remaining coconut milk and cook gently over a saucepan of simmering water, stirring constantly until it is thick enough to coat the back of a spoon.

4. Remove from the heat and cool. Whip the cream until soft peaks form, then stir in the cooled custard.

5. Chop a little of the mango into small pieces and purée the remainder in a food processor or push through a sieve.

6. Fold the mango purée and chopped mango into the custard. Pour into a shallow, freezerproof dish and freeze until slushy.

7. Remove from the freezer and process in the food processor, or beat with an electric whisk until smooth. Freeze and beat once more then transfer to a freezer container and cover with a lid. Freeze until solid.

8. Remove the ice cream about 20-30 minutes before serving and allow to soften in the refrigerator. Scoop into dishes and serve sprinkled with toasted flaked almonds.

Step 2 Beat together the egg yolks and sugar in a bowl. Add a few tablespoons of the hot coconut milk and stir well.

Step 3 Cook the custard over a saucepan of simmering water, stirring constantly, until it coats the back of a spoon.

Step 6 Fold the mango purée and chopped mango into the custard.

Cook's Notes

Time
Preparation takes 30 minutes and cooking takes 10 minutes. Freezing takes several hours.

Preparation
Do not allow the coconut milk to boil or the eggs will curdle when added.

Cook's Tip
Beating the ice cream as it freezes breaks up the ice crystals and gives it a smoother texture.

BANANAS IN COCONUT MILK

If you can get the small, firm Thai bananas, increase the
cooking time so that the banana is cooked until just tender.

SERVES 6

2½ cups thin coconut milk
4 tbsps sugar
Pinch of salt
6 small unripe bananas
Toasted unsweetened shredded coconut, to decorate

1. Combine the coconut milk, sugar and salt in a wok or
saucepan and heat gently, stirring until the sugar
dissolves. Bring to the boil and boil rapidly for 5
minutes.

2. Cut the bananas in half or into chunks and place in
the coconut milk. Reduce the heat and simmer gently

Step 1 Bring the
mixture to the boil
and boil rapidly for 5
minutes.

for 2-3 minutes or until the bananas are just soft.

3. Allow the mixture to cool and serve slightly warm or
chilled, sprinkled with the coconut.

Step 1 Combine the
milk, sugar and salt
in a wok and heat
gently, stirring until
the sugar dissolves.

Step 2 Add the
banana chunks to the
coconut milk and
simmer for 2-3
minutes or until the
bananas are just soft.

Cook's Notes

Time
Preparation takes 10 minutes
and cooking takes 12 minutes.

Buying Guide
Buy slightly green bananas for
this dish.

TAPIOCA WITH GOLDEN THREADS

Golden threads are used to decorate desserts. Tapioca is a starch from the root of the cassava tree. It can be found at Oriental stores.

SERVES 6

Golden Threads
6 egg yolks
1¼ cups water
1¼ cups sugar

Tapioca
2½ cups thin coconut milk
3 tbsps pearl tapioca, rinsed
1 tbsp palm sugar

1. To make the golden threads, puncture the base of a paper or plastic cup 3 or 4 times with a knitting needle or skewer.

2. Stir the egg yolks together and leave in the refrigerator until required.

3. Place the water and sugar in a wok or saucepan and heat, stirring until the sugar dissolves. Bring to the boil, then reduce the heat to maintain a gentle boil.

4. Pour about one-third to a half of the egg yolk mixture into the cup whilst holding it over the saucepan of sugar and water. Let the yolks flow through the holes in the cup, in a steady stream. Move the cup slowly, from side to side so that the yolks form strings.

5. As the yolk mixture hits the water it will cook. When set, remove it with a skewer, fold into bundles, and place on a plate. Repeat with the remaining egg, and chill until required.

6. To make the tapioca, place the coconut milk and tapioca in a saucepan and stir in the sugar. Cook over a low heat for 30 minutes, stirring occasionally until the

Step 1 Puncture the base of a paper or plastic cup 3 or 4 times.

Step 4 Pour one-third of the egg yolk mixture into the cup, whilst holding it over the saucepan of sugar and water. Let the yolks flow through the holes in a steady stream, moving cup slowly so that the yolks form strings.

Step 5 When the ribbons of egg yolk are set, remove with a skewer and fold into bundles.

tapioca is soft. Spoon into dishes and arrange the golden threads on top.

Cook's Notes

Time
Preparation takes 20 minutes and cooking takes 45 minutes.

Serving Idea
Serve any spare golden threads with coffee.

Index